D0733623

WITHDRAWN

UNSTUCK

52 WAYS TO GET AND KEEP YOUR
CREATIVITY FLOWING
AT HOME, AT WORK &
IN YOUR STUDIO

NOAH SCALIN

IF FOUND, PLEASE RETURN THIS BOOK TO

Voyageur Press

DEDICATION

For Jessica, who said "yes."

First published in 2011 by Voyageur Press, an imprint of MBI Publishing Company, 400 First Avenue North, Suite 300, Minneapolis, MN 55401 USA

Voyageur Press titles are also available at discounts in bulk quantity for industrial or sales-promotional use. For details write to Special Sales Manager at MBI Publishing Company, 400 First Avenue North, Suite 300, Minneapolis, MN 55401 USA.

To find out more about our books, visit us online at www.voyageurpress.com.

Library of Congress Cataloging-in-Publication Data

Scalin, Noah.
 Unstuck : 52 ways to get (and keep) your creativity flowing / Noah Scalin.
    p. cm.
 ISBN 978-0-7603-4134-6 (flexibound)
 1. Creative ability—Problems, exercises, etc. 2. Creative thinking—Problems, exercises, etc. I. Title.
 BF408.S297 2011
 153.3'5—dc22
                              2011007648

Edited by Danielle Ibister
Design Manager: Katie Sonmor
Designed by Noah Scalin
Layout by Karl Laun

Printed in China
10 9 8 7 6 5 4 3 2 1

CONTENTS

Peleg Top is a master business and personal development coach. He mentors creative entrepreneurs on how to make serious money, become better leaders, and create the life and business they desire. A designer at heart with over twenty years of experience running his own successful creative agency, Peleg is a national speaker and an author of fine design and marketing books.

FOREWORD

I like to think that being stuck is actually a good place to be.
As a creative person, stuck isn't where I want to spend all my time, but I've come to regard that stuck feeling as a friend, not an enemy. When I'm stuck, I read it as a helpful warning sign that I'm not paying attention. Being stuck reminds me to be purposeful again in maintaining my creativity energy. Being stuck is a signal that I am not in a state of flow.

Getting stuck, occasionally, is a natural part of creativity. It happens to the best of us. In every creative person's life, we arrive occasionally at a place where creativity stops flowing. For a while we're happily riding a creative wave and then out of the blue—nothing. For a terrifying few hours (or days, or weeks), we think the next idea will never come. We become afraid that our ideas are not good enough and probably never really were good enough. At worst, some of us just give up completely.

Stuck happens. Unfortunately, with all our formal education and lifelong, on-the-job training, we seldom learn how to get unstuck from the stuck places we find ourselves. That's what this book is about. Instead of just repeating the same old techniques that didn't work before, over and over, and expecting them to somehow work differently now, here are some different ideas to help us actually do something different.

Creativity is a natural part of being. We were born creative. As kids, we were not afraid to create. We lived a freely creative life. But as we grow older, we lose the necessary space in our lives for creativity to flow. We become occupied with the responsibilities of adulthood and we let our creativity get shoved to the side. We lose our flow.

This book can help you step back into your natural state of flow. The exercises and ideas presented in the following pages are designed to get you out of your routine. This is not a book you should simply read; it's an action book with effective recipes to shake your patterns and spark new ideas that will move whatever you are doing forward.

Creativity is always, by its nature, unknown territory. And for even the most adventuresome explorers of creativity, the unknown can get scary. When you lose your nerve, and when it seems you've turned one way and your flow has turned off a different way, this book can be your companion back on to the safe path through the unknown. The techniques and projects are simple and effective. With the right guide, the unknown can be exciting without being scary.

There is a big payoff for doing this work. Besides becoming more confident as you experience your creative genius returning, you will start noticing how other, unrelated areas in your life that were also stuck (perhaps some areas you weren't paying much attention to) will start opening up and getting back into their flow as well. That's the magic that you can tap into with this work. Once your flow is unstuck, you can't stop it or tell where else in your life it will have an effect. Just enjoy the ride.

Back in flow, what you thought were dead ends can suddenly become the trailheads of new paths. Think of this book as a collection of doorways opening into rooms or wide landscapes you have yet to discover. Each doorway is a new passage to lead you back to your flow, a passage leading you back to your natural creative self.

So congratulations to you on feeling stuck. Lucky you. You've been handed a helpful sign that tells you something in your creative life needs shaking up. Take the sign seriously, but don't panic. Here's a friendly book that will take you by the shoulders and start the shaking.

Peleg Top
Los Angeles
March 2011
www.PelegTop.com

Peleg Top. *photo: Jeff Zander*

5

GENERATING YOUR OWN CREATIVE ENERGY

This book is a box of tools for your brain.

Has your creative engine stalled out? Don't worry, you're in good company. Everyone needs a creative tune-up from time to time, and this book is your personal toolkit for getting the gears unstuck.

I have a full-time creative job, which means that I can't wait for inspiration to strike. I have to make it happen myself every day. One way I filled up my own creative toolbox was to do a yearlong daily creative project I called Skull-A-Day (www.skulladay.com). I spent that year learning a lot of amazing lessons that I have applied to my work and life every day since. But I know it's not realistic to ask you to embark on a long creative process when you need results right now, so I'm going to let you borrow some of my tools.

This book contains a collection of projects that I've gathered and developed over the years. They are meant to spark your brain and get it moving again right away. From games played by artists of the last century to exercises my friends have recently taught me, there is something in here for you regardless of your circumstances or skill level. There are even interviews with some of my favorite creative people about how they've dealt with their own creative roadblocks.

With a bit of practice, anyone can start generating more energy to get their creative engine running again smoothly and out of the repair shop for a long time to come.

382. Pumpkin Anatomy Skull
Even though I finished my yearlong Skull-A-Day project, I still make skulls from time to time because I enjoy the positive feedback of sharing my work. After I posted this pumpkin I carved for Halloween, people immediately started sending me images of ones they were inspired to make because of it!

WHO NEEDS CREATIVE INSPIRATION?
i.e., Who is this book for?

The real question should be "Who doesn't need it?!"

Obviously, people in a whole host of creative jobs (architecture, graphic design, fashion, theater, film, photography, writing, music) need help from time to time when they just aren't feeling inspired. Heck, there were times when I was writing this book that I wished it had come out already so I could've turned to it for help!

But what if you're not doing a creative job? The reality is that people need creative thinking at every stage in their lives and in every field of work. Whether you're a student stuck on a homework assignment or a businessperson trying to find new revenue streams, a teacher looking to inspire new ways of thinking or a scientist looking for better solutions to old problems, the tools used for developing creative thinking can help you discover unexpected answers. And certainly when times are hard and money is tight, new ideas can be some of the most valuable commodities around.

Yet for too many people, creativity can seem like something completely ephemeral—a thing that comes and goes with no rhyme or reason. And the assumption is that if you've hit a roadblock along a creative path you just have to wait around and eventually, if you're lucky, a good idea will strike you and then the creative process can restart. Nothing could be further from the truth.

The reality is that there are good ideas and exciting possibilities all around us all of the time. But it takes practice to recognize the creative opportunities that exist. Just like practicing the piano or working out at a gym, the more you do it the better you'll become. In fact it may help to think of the exercises in this book as just that, physical exercises for your brain. They range from stretches to warm-ups to full workouts, and they're just as important for you as the ones you do with the rest of your body.

111. Newspaper Skull
My sister kindly posed for me in an outdoor café in New York City to get this shot. We had fun watching to see if passers discovered that it wasn't just a normal paper being read. Realistically, most people aren't paying that much attention to the details of the world around them, so it's easier than you'd think to get away with some odd behavior.

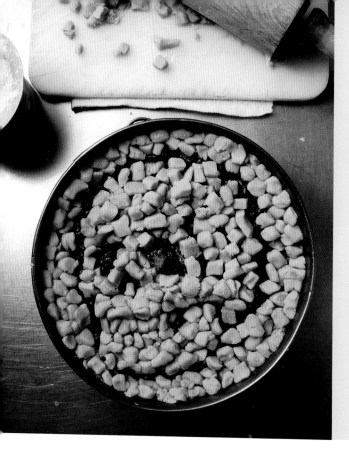

362. Pie Skull
By constantly talking about my Skull-A-Day project with everyone I came in contact with, all kinds of interesting opportunities came up. In this case the owner of Ipanema, one of my favorite local restaurants, gave me access to their kitchen and let me take part in making one of their signature pies! I even got to see it being eaten by the patrons after it was done.

HOW TO USE THIS BOOK

The projects contained within are not about a specific tangible outcome but rather about causing your brain to jump out of the groove it's been caught in. The idea is to do a task that will cause your thinking to move sideways and open you up to new opportunities and ideas that have been waiting to be discovered right next to where you're looking now!

Nothing is set in stone. Always feel free to change the directions I've provided as the spirit calls you. If the title of a project inspires you, but you come up with a better way to do it, try it out! However, if you find something is frightening to you, definitely give it a try first. That's usually a sign that it's a lesson you especially need to learn! The potential positive outcomes are well worth the small risks you take here.

There are several ways to start:

- If you know you have a specific amount of time to get motivated, choose a project based on where it's situated in the book—from 30-second projects at the front to multi-hour projects at the back.
- You can decide whether you want to do something that will get you out of your workspace or that allows you to stay there.
- You can pick projects that require other people to participate or that you can do alone.
- You can select projects based on the lessons (see pages 12–15) you want to practice more.
- Or you can always just flip to a random page!

A NOTE ON TIME

The amounts of time listed for each project are not necessarily literal. They're meant to help you allocate a set amount of creative time in your day. Definitely don't feel obliged to stick with the suggested times, especially if you find yourself having fun doing a project and wanting more!

For me, having a strict deadline is one of the best motivating factors in getting creative work done. I have a very hard time getting motivated if I know there's no urgency. If that sounds like you, definitely use the time allotted as your guides and set a timer to make sure you stick with it!

ICONS

Each project features a handy sidebar that gives you some key details about the project at a glance.

WHERE

Many of the projects can be done anywhere you would like, indoors or out. Why not try them in usual places like on a bus or in a restaurant?

Some of the projects are best done in/near your workspace so you can have access to specific materials.

Several projects require that you go out of your workspace, and specifically outside, to get them done.

SKILLS

These icons represent "The Big Seven" and are explained in detail on pages 12–15.

EXTRAS

While most projects can be done by yourself, or with others, these require additional people to make them happen.

These require the use of a camera. A cellphone camera is sufficient.

THE BIG SEVEN

The projects in this book can help you learn the seven big lessons I taught myself during my year of making skulls:

1. Let Go of Preciousness. Probably one of the biggest creative stumbling blocks is our need for getting things right. And believe me, I'm a perfectionist myself, so I know how hard it is to let that go. The reality is that treating your creations as precious little things to protect keeps you from the world of possibilities that comes from trying new things out, making mistakes, and getting things wrong.

2. Freedom Comes from Limitations. If someone were to give me an infinite amount of time and an unlimited budget to create something, I would be frozen. It's only from narrowing down the options that creativity becomes possible, as you are forced to push against the walls that close you in.

3. Get Out of Your Environment. No matter how inspiring your workspace is, there's only so much creative work that can be done within it. Of course if you're in a place that's not so inspiring to begin with, the need to be elsewhere is even more urgent. And since most people spend the majority of their time indoors, they're missing out on the much wider world right outside their door.

Let Go of Preciousness
3. Sir-Skull-A-Day

I waited to share my daily project until the third day in, which is when I created this piece out of a cassette tape I found in my basement. And even though I didn't think it was the best thing I'd ever made, I took the risk and put it out there anyway. And surprisingly, the reaction was way more positive than I expected!

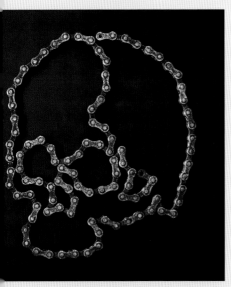

Freedom Comes from Limitations
267. Skull Chain (Gang)

Over the course of my project I cultivated a skill I call "finding the skull within." Basically, I use the limitations of the material to drive my creative process. In this case there was a limited length to the bicycle chain, and I knew that the line could not cross over itself. Once I made one version of a skull, I was inspired to see if I could make others, each with increasing difficulty.

Get Out of Your Environment
321. Junkyard Skull

Nothing gets the creative juices flowing like getting out of the office to do something out of the ordinary; and making art in the middle of a junkyard definitely qualifies. I'm hoping the people who later discovered this piece, which I made by bending the fins of this car's radiator, had a bit of an out-of-the-ordinary experience as well!

4. Get Out of Your Comfort Zone. At some point in our lives we've probably been told not to make a fool of ourselves, but the fact is that's one of the most effective ways to get creative inspiration! Fear of rejection and fear of embarrassment—these are the ephemeral enemies of creativity.

5. Get Things by Giving Them Away. It may sound counterintuitive, but you get a lot from giving things away. If I had kept my own project under wraps rather than sharing it as I went along, I probably would have had one-tenth of the good experiences that came out of it. The more I gave away, the more people gave back to me.

6. Collaborate. There's no substitute for the benefits you get when working creatively with other people. Some of the best things I got out of doing my own project were the wonderful new friendships and the deepening of my existing friendships that came from incorporating other people into my work. You get results that are exponentially greater when you don't just work alone.

7. Inspiration Is Everywhere. You may have heard it before, but it's not until you really start looking around in a panic for solutions that you discover how true it is. Inspiration really is everywhere. And once you start practicing, the ability to find ideas in even the most mundane environments gets easier and easier.

Get Out of Your Comfort Zone
230. NYC Trash Skull
The majority of the pieces I created for Skull-A-Day were purely temporary—only existing long enough for me to document them—and then were dismantled or left behind for others to discover. This piece had me digging in a New York City trash can, which is definitely something I would not normally be willing to do if I hadn't committed to getting something done every day!

Get Things by Giving Them Away
319. Two-Part Stencil Skull
I made several stencils in the course of my Skull-A-Day project, which I then gave away as free patterns so people could make their own skulls. The only thing I asked is that people showed me what they did with the stencils. Not only have people sent me images, but I've even been given gifts made with them and made new friends because of them. I've definitely gotten much more from sharing them than I would have by keeping them to myself.

Collaborate
342. (Band of The) Hand Skull
Collaborating with friends gave me opportunities to create things I never would have otherwise, plus the time spent with them was way more interesting than if I had just gone to dinner or a movie with them. In this case my friend Madonna got her belly dance troupe to give me a literal hand in making this piece!

Inspiration Is Everywhere
257. Little Did They Know Skull
Can you see the skull hiding in this picture? (If not, try turning the book upside down.) I've passed by this wall thousands of times over the years, but it was only when I had honed my ability to find inspiration everywhere that I finally saw the skull that had been staring at me all along.

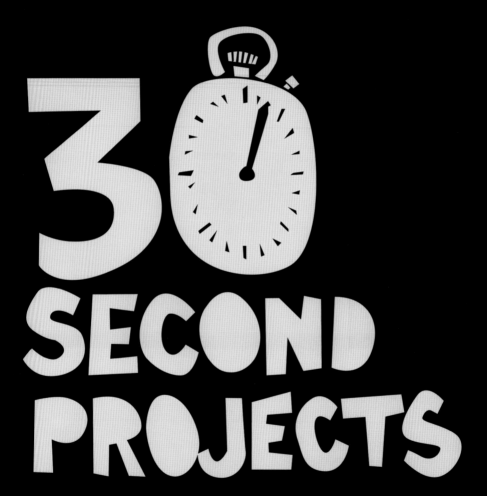

EYE SPY

Very often the best way to get out of a creative rut is to do something completely unrelated to the task at hand. The momentary pause gives your brain a chance to reset and find new pathways to the solution. It's even better if the moment you take involves some laughter or at least a smile. The simple act of adding eyes to everyday objects and surfaces in your environment can lead to some unexpected amusement that could be just what the doctor ordered.

HOW TO DO IT:

1. Cut out a pair of eyes provided in the back of the book on pages 231–235 (or cut them all out in advance and keep them in a jar or bag for use at a moment's notice).

2. Look around your immediate environment for something that has the potential to be a face. Pretty much any horizontal line can be seen as a mouth.

3. Tape or glue your eyes to the object or surface and step back to enjoy. Even better, call other people over and enjoy their response.

4. Leave the eyes for someone else to discover later.

ALTERNATIVE: Make your own eyes or buy googly eyes from a craft store and keep on hand.

BONUS: Make up a story about the character you just created.

30 SECOND PROJECTS

Where did you put your eyes?

How did people respond?

DO A 180

One of the easiest ways to reignite creativity is to get a new perspective on things. And the best way to get a new perspective is to do so literally. Sometimes making the slightest shift is enough to notice something you've been missing or to think about it differently.

HOW TO DO IT:

1. Take whatever you are working on at the moment and turn it (45, 90, or 180 degrees) and continue to work on it this way for the next thirty seconds.
2. Using the space at right, document what you did and how it affected your work.

If you're doing a task that doesn't seem to allow for this, figure out a way to make it work (i.e., if you can't rotate your screen, turn yourself!).

ALTERNATIVE: Work in front of a mirror, keeping your eyes on the version of it in the mirror.

What happened when you changed your perspective?

ACRONYM

Another Creative Resource, Only Needs Your Mother?
Artists' Crazy Relatives Of Nearly Yawning Moods?
Acceptable Colors: Red, Orange, Navy, Yellow, Maroon?

Did you know that the words "laser" and "scuba" were originally acronyms? SCUBA stood for Self-Contained Underwater Breathing Apparatus and LASER stood for Light Amplification by Stimulated Emission of Radiation, but now they've become words in their own right. This exercise gets your creative wheels turning by playing with the potential within the words around you.

HOW TO DO IT:

1. Choose a word from the list provided, or start with a word of your choosing.
2. Don't spend too long thinking. Just pick a word that starts with one of the letters within the word and write it down in the space next to it.
3. Work around that first word to quickly create the rest of the acronym. It doesn't have to be good or even vaguely relate to the word's meaning. The idea is to do this fast to build up your skill at thinking on the spot.

BONUS: Illustrate the acronym you've created.

ALTERNATIVE: See how many different results you can come up with for the same word.

W.O.R.K. S.P.A.C.E.

WORD LIST:

DONUT

BOING

GLOB

FLIPPANT

NEATO

TOOT

SKITTER

PUMPERNICKLE

AARDVARK

BLASTOFF

GIBLETS

TEEPEE

DIPTHONG

LUNKHEAD

SKULL

WALNUT

SPAM

ELBOW

BANJO

LUTE

CORNPONE

UNDERPANTS

DOODLE

YOGURT

SALIVA

IT'S A LONG STORY

One of my favorite things to do with kids is have them tell me the story of their favorite book or movie. The scenes and lines of dialogue they focus on and prioritize are fascinating and often quite entertaining. Their succinct versions of long and complicated stories are often more interesting than the source material.

This task requires you to think like one of those kids. Developing the ability to quickly get to the essence of what is important to you about something can really help you when you need to be creative on the fly.

HOW TO DO IT:
1. Pick one of your favorite movies or books.
2. Time yourself and try to tell as clear a version of it as you can in under thirty seconds. You may want to give this a couple of tries to really get it down.
3. Write the resulting story in the space provided so you can return to it and give it another try from time to time.

Once upon a time . . .

BONUS: Create something inspired by your condensed story. It could be a sequential illustration, an animated film, a dramatic reading, or even a puppet show!

ALTERNATIVE: See if you can tell it in ten seconds. How about five seconds? Is it possible to make a one-second version?

ANDY STEFANOVICH advises people at some of the largest corporations in the world about creativity.

IT'S ALL ABOUT WORDS

Having been in the creativity and innovation world for more than twenty years, I feel as though I've seen nearly every point-of-view around "creating." I've become most fascinated by the simple use of language as an onramp to getting unstuck. It is, in my view, an elevated approach to unleashing the genius in all of us. Elegant. Simple. And the belief that words can change the world.

1. Context to Create

Too often, we plunge into the creative objective without the fullest level of context. What strategies, themes, trends, or insights can inform our creative thinking? It's asking, "What new context could inform our thinking that we have not considered?" Insert it and watch the energy increase around the ideas. Constantly ebbing and flowing in and out of a context to create will drive new and powerful thinking.

2. The Bigger Big

If you are working in service of a big objective, make it bigger. If the objective is about reaching a million people with your idea, make it a billion, as an optic, and see how it shifts your perspective and unleashes new ideas.

> *"I've become most fascinated by the simple use of language as an onramp to getting unstuck."*

3. Create and Lead

When working with high concepts, look to demystify them. In this case, I've simplified the notion of entrepreneurship into "create and lead." People know how to create in their mind and lead with their actions, but they may not know how to access the idea of entrepreneurship. It's about making the idea accessible.

4. Stop, Start, Continue

It's not do, do, do, more, more, more. Too often we look only to grow an idea continually. Instead, try evaluating the merits of the idea, then "growing" only where it's best, starting to grow in new places, and/or stopping altogether in other places. When stuck, ask yourself, "What should I stop doing, start doing, and continue doing?" Not growing an idea might grow it.

So there are four new frames to unleash your thinking. Simple language that inspires and engages the mind. Words do, in fact, create the world.

*Chief Curator and Provocateur at Prophet, **Andy Stefanovich** has earned a reputation as one of the most disruptive and effective advisors in business. He has spent the past twenty years helping companies like GE and Disney drive innovation from the inside out. Andy is passionate about books (especially kids' books) and their impact on the world. His first book,* Look at More, *is a guide to innovation, growth, and change.*

www.prophet.com/lookatmore

IONIC, DORIC, OR CORINTHIAN?

Sometimes we're too caught up in things having to go together in one specific way. One simple method I use for generating new ideas is a mix-and-match column approach to the key words of a project. All of the variations can be tested out until you find one that sparks an idea.

HOW TO DO IT:

1. In the space provided, write one of the major themes that is important to the work you're currently doing at the top of each column. (I've done a sample one so you can get a feel for it.)
2. Under each theme, write a list of adjectives that relate to it.
3. Choose one item from each column and write it down in the space provided. Continue mixing and matching all of the various words. Note any particularly interesting or unusual associations that stand out to you.

BONUS: Try drawing or writing something based on your favorite associations before you get back to work.

ALTERNATIVE: Do a three- or four-column version with additional themes and more complex interactions.

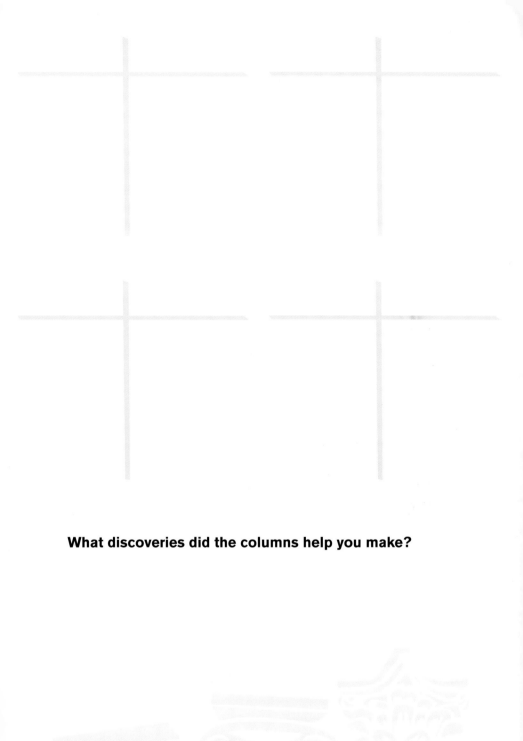

What discoveries did the columns help you make?

HAIKU EVERYWHERE

Not everyone is a poet, but everyone can write a haiku, and it can be done just about everywhere! This traditional form of non-rhyming Japanese poetry is usually written with seventeen syllables in English, which are broken into three lines (five, seven, and five syllables per line, respectively). Initially haiku were about nature, but modern ones can be on any topic. Their brevity encourages condensing complex thoughts and emotions into simple, elegant forms. While you could take hours to compose one, the goal of this exercise is to do it within a thirty-second time limit to help hone quick visual and mental interpretation reflexes. I've written hundreds of haiku, and not only did they give me a nice bit of quick creative satisfaction, but I was able to mine them later as source material for creative projects.

HOW TO DO IT

1. Use whatever you're working on at the moment as your inspiration. Alternately: Use anything that you can see at the moment.

2. Say your thoughts out loud while counting the syllables on your fingers. Remember, it's five, then seven, then five again. You can do this in your head if you're somewhere that talking out loud is inappropriate, but it does help to vocalize your thoughts.

3. Don't be critical of the results. Just keep adjusting the words to get it short enough to fit the format and then write it down!

4. Put your favorites in the space provided so you can return to them from time to time.

Haiku here . . .

HINT: The tricky part is finding the right word to fit the syllables remaining. This is a great time to start boning up on synonyms in your handy thesaurus! Use a real book as an excuse to get away from the computer if you're on one all day.

Haiku here . . .

BONUS: If you're done before thirty seconds are up, try seeing how many haiku you can make in that time on the same subject!

HAIKU-A-DAY

My friend Jennifer Willis has chosen to write a haiku a day for a year! Here are a few examples of how she translated everyday experiences with the form.

Hockey night again.
The arena is cold, but
the players are hot!

My handwriting was
once lovely, easy to read.
Now it's all just scrawl.

Now I've lost my voice.
I sound like a muppet or
cartoon character.

Stuck inside for days,
recovering from the flu,
bored out of my mind.

Check out all of Jennifer's haiku here:
www.jennifer-willis.com/topics/365-haiku

SIX-WORD MEMOIR

From Larry Smith, founder of SMITH *Magazine, the online community obsessed with personal storytelling and home of the Six-Word Memoir project and book series. www.smithmag.net.*

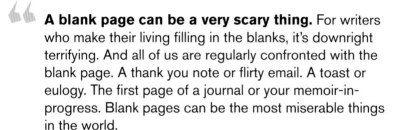

A blank page can be a very scary thing. For writers who make their living filling in the blanks, it's downright terrifying. And all of us are regularly confronted with the blank page. A thank you note or flirty email. A toast or eulogy. The first page of a journal or your memoir-in-progress. Blank pages can be the most miserable things in the world.

30 SECOND PROJECTS

Playing off a literary legend that Hemingway was once challenged to write a whole novel in just six words ("For sale: baby shoes, never worn"), *SMITH* decided to give the six-word challenge a personal twist. We asked our readers: How would you describe your life in exactly six words? We called it the "Six-Word Memoir." More than 400,000 Six-Word Memoirs later, people can't get enough of the form.

Larry Smith. *photo: Abigail Pope*

Why does it work? In part because it's so simple. Fear subsides when you chip away at the blank page one word at a time (and it's filled in just six). Don't like what you've come up with? Who cares? Start over. Or just keep writing more. It also works because anyone can do it. Across world in schools, churches, therapy groups, and even speed dating sessions, the Six-Word Memoir has become a creative catalyst—a kickstarter to break the mind's ice.

If I've learned one thing in a career consumed with doing just one thing, it's this: Everyone has a story. Whether you're Stephen Colbert ("Well, I thought it was funny") or my nephew Noah ("Eight years old, combed hair twice"), your story should be told. Six words is a way in.

HOW TO DO IT:

1. Take a few moments to think about what is important to you about your life right now.

2. Use the space provided to write about yourself or your current situation in just six words. Don't worry about being perfect.
You can do this over and over. Just get some words on paper.

3. Return to this page and add new stories when the mood strikes.

BONUS: Share your six words with *SMITH Magazine*'s community of storytellers at www.sixwordmemoirs.com.

What six words did you choose?

1   2   3   4   5   6

1   2   3   4   5   6

1   2   3   4   5   6

1   2   3   4   5   6

1   2   3   4   5   6

1   2   3   4   5   6

1   2   3   4   5   6

BONUS: Illustrate your story visually.

1   2   3   4   5   6

1   2   3   4   5   6

1   2   3   4   5   6

1   2   3   4   5   6

1   2   3   4   5   6

Six Tips for Writing Six-Word Memoirs

1. Be Specific.
"Dorothy Gale had the right idea."
"Quietly cultivating my inner Lynda Carter."

"Dorothy Gale" is much shorter than "iconic fictional girl who enjoyed many adventures but would prefer to end up back on the farm." "Lynda Carter" conjures up better imagery than, say, "strong beauty."

2. Be Honest.
"Girlfriend is pregnant, my husband said."
"Being a monk stunk. Better gay."

Many of the most interesting six-word memoirs are so real and raw that you begin to feel real emotions for people you've never met, much like a fictional character in a book you love.

3. Write Like You Talk.
"Barrister, barista, what's the diff, mom?"
"Wasn't born a redhead; fixed that."

These six-worders are great because you can hear the writers saying them to you. Forget the thesaurus and just use words that feel like your words.

4. Experiment with Structure.
"ABCs. MTV. SATs. THC. IRA. NPR."
"Caring for parents. Life is circular."

Six is a great number because of all the ways you can mix and match the form. Repetition can be powerful, and punctuation is your friend.

5. Tell a Story.
"Bachelor party. YouTube video. Wedding cancelled."
"Ex-wife and contractor now have house."

You can, in fact, tell a whole story—your story—in just six words. The best Six-Word Memoirs have a true narrative arc.

6. Be Yourself.
"Big hair, big heart, big hurry."
"Screw diabetes, pass me another cookie."

Don't try so hard! These aren't epic novels or Supreme Court decisions. Just start scribbling and see what catches your eye. It's your story, just go forth and tell it!

TWO
MINUTE
PROJECTS

ROLL THE DICE

Very often the most inspiring moments are the ones that happen completely randomly. However, if you're in the same environment day in and day out, the potential for random moments grows smaller and smaller. If getting out of your environment isn't an option and you don't have time to wait around for something to fly through the window, why not create a bit of chaos of your own? By rolling dice you introduce the unexpected into any situation.

SKILLS

In the back of the book on pages 231–235, you'll find three unusual dice to cut out and make yourself. Just follow the diagrams and leave these on your desk or wherever you find yourself most stuck; then you'll be ready to do this exercise whenever you need it! You can even throw them in your pocket or bag so they're with you all the time.

TWO
MINUTE
PROJECTS

HOW TO DO IT:

1. Roll the dice. There are 216 possible outcomes!

2. Document the results in the space provided.

3. Interpret the words in terms of the situation you're dealing with now. You can try to incorporate all three together, or just use one or two if you're particularly inspired.

4. Take an action based on the results, whether it's making something new or taking an existing project in a new direction. Even if it seems ridiculous to do it, give it a try just to have the outcome be different than what you had previously been doing.

5. Record the action and results so you can return to the ones that were especially effective.

NOTE: Extra time required to prepare for this project.

What did the dice tell you to do?

How did you follow their directions?

ALTERNATIVE: Instead of using the preprinted side of the dice, make them inside out and write or draw your own details on them. Consider using language that is specific to the type of work you do.

KHYAL™ is a designer, artist, writer, photographer, and illustrator.

A CONVEYOR BELT OF CREATIVITY

Creativity can be like the cartoon Tasmanian Devil, whirling you around like a wild machine of productivity. And then, just as suddenly, it can slam the door in your face.

Because of this, I've developed some personal techniques for dealing with nonproductive states that realign my focus and grease the creativity wheel.

1. Have multiple projects going at all times.

I have lots of creative outlets: design, writing, illustration, painting, sculpture, photography, apparel design, and more. I also collaborate with my designer husband on interior projects, furniture design, and creating and executing design events, along with pop-up stores and galleries.

2. Have a daily plan of attack.

I update my short list of client deadlines daily. Added to that are personal projects, which include art and design shows and events. I add these to the two other commitments I've made to myself: A) to create a new digital drawing of my character The Weather sKwirl™ each day and post it to my weatherskwirl.com blog, and B) to research, write, and post a new entry every other day at DesignerGrill.com, a daily art and design blog I share with my husband.

> **"...if I am not feeling happy and productive within a few minutes, I move on."**

photos: kHyal™

3. Execute in a way that helps you do your very best work.

My clients always come first so I begin each day with my list of client assignments. However, if I sit down to deploy a project and feel stuck, bored, lost, or traumatized by it, I move on to another item on my list that appeals to my current state of mind. I might paint the trim in my studio that I've been putting off, which is a physical activity; or I might write a blog post I know is due— something that keeps me sitting at my desk but is more freeing intellectually.

Whatever I choose, if I am not feeling happy and productive within a few minutes, I move on—the idea being that I cycle through my desires and responsibilities to find my best self and don't waste time on things that aren't working.

4. The end result.

Compelling, successful client and personal work. Happy clients. Happy self. No wasted time. A conveyor belt of creativity.

kHyal™ *has exhibited her work in the American Visionary Art Museum, the Housatonic Art Museum, the New Britain Museum of American Art, the Outsider Art Fair, Intuit, the Cooper Union, and galleries from New York to London. kHyal founded fiZz Agency and cofounded PUSH Workshops in 2007, talentEd in 2008, and DesignerGrill in 2009. She is the creator of The Weather sKwirl™ and BlipWorld and is a member of the Women's Internet History Project. kHyal lives and works in Black Rock, Connecticut, with her designer husband, Karl; her computer-crazed networking expert son, Tyler; and her two cats, Scootie and Squeaks.*

www.getfizz.com

CREATIVE ADVICE

DOODLE DANDY

If you want to be ready for being creative whenever and wherever, it's important to develop the ability to see the potential in everything. Children have done this activity for ages, but how many people try it again later in life? Don't worry about making art. The key is to just get your brain turning and your hand moving.

TWO MINUTE PROJECTS

HOW TO DO IT:

1. Choose a squiggle (or create one of your own in the space provided).

2. Use a phrase from the list below (or create one of you own).

3. Using whatever tools you like, transform the squiggle into a doodle that visually expresses the phrase in some way. It could be literal or just a response to the phrase.

PHRASE LIST

Happy as a clam
I can't get no satisfaction
Where in the world?
A hard day's night
Human nature
Is there a doctor in the house?
The art of noise
Here comes trouble
Abracadabra!
What's that sound?

The birds and the bees
When pigs fly
Lost in translation
They might be giants
No bones about it
You are what you eat
A new hope
Everything you know is wrong
A blessing in disguise
Don't panic

Get doodling . . .

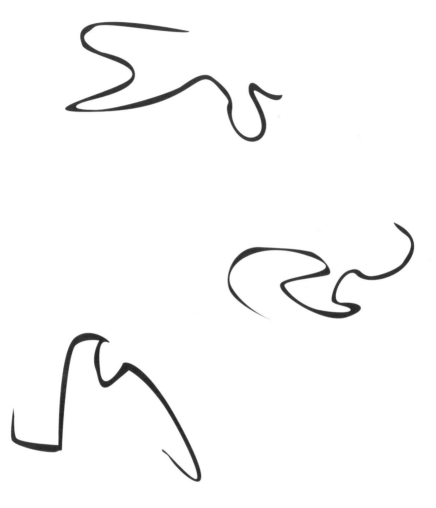

ALTERNATIVE: Have someone else create the squiggle and suggest the subject matter for you.

SQUIGGLE CHAMPION OF THE WORLD

Artist Matthew Lively has been declared the "Squiggle Champion of the World." Working with squiggles and suggestions provided by strangers, he has transformed hundreds of random lines into clever illustrations.

See Matt's non-squiggle art at: **www.matthewlively.com**

Freedom Comes from Limitations. *image: Matthew Lively*

Let Go of Preciousness. *image: Matthew Lively*

BEFORE

AFTER

image: Matthew Lively

Get Out of Your Comfort Zone. *image: Matthew Lively*

INSPIRATION

Keep doodling . . .

THOUGHT BUBBLES

It's very easy to get stuck in your own head when you're trying to be creative, so it's important to spend some time in others' heads from time to time. This simple exercise is all about getting your imagination working by making interior monologues visual.

HOW TO DO IT:

1. Clip out one or more of the thought bubbles provided in the back of the book on pages 231–235 (or make your own).

2. Tape or glue the thought bubbles to images or objects. This could be in a magazine, on photos in your living space or working space, or even on physical items you encounter out and about.*

3. Add a short message or image that reveals what the person or object is thinking about.

4. Use the space at right to document what you did with your bubbles.

5. Leave them for others to discover.

*If you do things in public, be sure not to be destructive of public or private property if you don't want to get accused of vandalism!

Where did you use your thought bubbles?

How did other people react?

photo: Ji Lee

INSPIRATION

Artist Ji Lee started the Bubble Project by making thousands of speech bubble stickers, which he placed on advertisements around New York City. The blank bubbles encouraged passersby to put in their own captions and created an interaction with what was previously a one-way medium. The project has now spread worldwide, and people are encouraged to download and make their own bubbles with a template provided online.

www.thebubbleproject.com

MEMORY MAPPING

Sometimes just getting your mind off the task at hand and intensely working on something unrelated is enough to start the juices flowing again. This task is partially about developing a sharp visual memory (which is great for recalling creative ideas when you've got to work quickly), but it's also a great chance to practice making up creative solutions when you don't know the answers.

TWO MINUTE PROJECTS

HOW TO DO IT:

1. Using one of the frames provided, quickly draw a map of all forty-eight contiguous states in America.
2. If you can't remember a state's shape, make something up instead.
3. Try to complete an entire map in the time allotted or just do as much as you can and return to it later.

BONUS: Add all of the states' names. And if you can't remember one, make it up.

ALTERNATIVE: For a greater challenge, create a continent or the entire globe from memory.

Feel free to add Alaska & Hawaii as well . . .

IT'S MY WORLD

In 2001, artist Graham Rawle created a series of limited-edition products he called Niff Actuals. Among them was a set of functional three-dimensional globes that were hand-painted from memory and called "It's My World."

photo: Graham Rawle

photo: Graham Rawle

Rawle has also created several excellent books using found objects and vintage texts as source materials. Get inspired by his works at:
www.grahamrawle.com

SEVEN THINGS

WHERE

SKILLS

Improvisation is really the name of the game when it comes to finding a creative spark. The ability to develop ideas on the fly is something that can be useful in almost any field. Who better to learn that skill from than improv performers? They have to be constantly on their toes as they create work instantaneously, using suggestions from the audience or each other. My friend Eliza Skinner, a comedian and writer known for her ability to create improvised musicals, shared this exercise, which she uses with her own improv students.

TWO MINUTE PROJECTS

HOW TO DO IT:

1. Choose one of the topics supplied.

2. Quickly write your answers in the spaces provided (or on your own paper). These aren't meant to be serious, so have fun with them. But be sure to keep track of your time and finish in two minutes or less. The key is pressure, so set a timer if need be!

3. Add your own topics once you've done a few of the ones provided.

BONUS: Illustrate or write a short story about one of the ideas you came up with.

ALTERNATIVE: Try this with a large group, taking turns with the same or different topics.

TOPICS (suggested by Eliza):

7 excuses to get out of a date that's going badly

7 names for a shrimp

7 worst imaginable cookie flavors

7 reasons to send back soup

7 sounds that a giraffe might make

7 secret nicknames for Robert DeNiro

7 titles for a love song to a snail

7 jobs an octopus would be terrible at

7 ways to unclog a drain

7 catch phrases for a detective

7 new moustache styles

7 names for new dance moves
(and descriptions for the moves)

Good things come in 7s . . .

Check out how Eliza Skinner puts her own finely honed improvisational skills to work at **www.ElizaSkinner.net.**

CHARLIE TODD founded the internationally known Improv Everywhere, which creates unusual experiences for unsuspecting audiences.

WALK, DON'T JUMP!

photo: Chad Nicholson

I work from home, so during cold New York weather it's possible for me to go a day or two without even going outside. When I find myself in a rut creatively, I know I need to venture out for a walk, blizzard be damned. The simple act of walking and observing the world around you can yield unexpected ideas. It's best if you're just walking to think, not to run an errand or accomplish any other task. A few years back, I was on one such walk in my neighborhood when I noticed a long, four-foot-tall ledge on the side of a building. I had walked by hundreds of times but had never really seen it.

I climbed up on top of it to get a new perspective. The act of standing on a ledge, no matter how short, put me in the mind of a suicide jumper. My mind started to race. What if I put a well-dressed man on this ledge in the middle of the day? What if I got together all of the usual elements of a suicide jump attempt here on this comically short ledge?

Improv Everywhere's Suicide Jumper project was born. A few weeks later, we staged a prank where my actor friend Will Hines stood on the ledge, looking like he was ready to end it all.

photo: Chad Nicholson

Soon after, a second actor dressed as a cop appeared and attempted to talk him out of it through a megaphone. A third actor jumped out of a cab to play the concerned wife, while a fourth appeared on the ledge as the jumper's coworker, trying to coax him back inside.

The absurd scene quickly drew a crowd of New Yorkers gawking and laughing at how seriously we were all treating it. Finally an actor dressed as a fireman appeared with a tiny trampoline. Will decided life was worth living after all and, after a tense pause, jumped to his safety. The crowd cheered, and all of the actors disappeared, leaving everyone behind to wonder what the hell just happened.

The resulting video was a hit, with 3.6 million views on YouTube to date. I still walk by the ledge on a regular basis, and each time I can't help but smile. There is a world of ideas hiding in plain sight. You just have to slow down and look for them.

Charlie Todd is the founder of Improv Everywhere. He has produced, directed, performed, and documented the group's work for more than nine years. He is also a teacher and performer of improvisation comedy at the Upright Citizens Brigade Theatre.

www.improveverywhere.com

"The simple act of walking and observing the world around you can yield unexpected ideas. "

CREATIVE ADVICE

CLOUD INVESTIGATOR

Spending time really paying attention to your environment is a great way to get out of a creative rut. Your task is to do this with intention and literally go looking for some inspiration. Everyone has spent some time looking at the clouds and discovering the images hidden within, but if you've started to see them as just clouds, this is for you.

HOW TO DO IT:

1. Head outside during the day and look up.
2. Find a cloud to work with. If there are no clouds outside, look for a tree or some other complex natural formation.
3. In the space provided, list as many things as you can see in the shape in two minutes. Try to come up with at least twenty!

BONUS: Choose one or more to illustrate or write a short story about.

What did you discover in the clouds?

IS IT BIGGER THAN A BREAD BOX?

What's holding you back? It's hard to answer straightforward questions about yourself or your situation creatively. We know what the answers should be, so we give them without thinking. But unusual questions give your mind a chance to play and possibly reveal some things you never knew about yourself or your work. If you're stuck on the obvious questions, this is a chance for your brain to switch gears.

HOW TO DO IT:

1. Take ten minutes to answer some of the questions below. You can even spend all of your time thoroughly answering just one. Feel free to use additional paper as needed. Some of these may seem ridiculous, but take them as seriously as you can. Flippant answers won't help you get unstuck.

2. Once you've written your answers, come back from time to time to see if you feel the same way or would say something different.

BONUS: Add your own questions—ones that you'd like to be asked or would like to ask others—in the blank spaces provided.

ALTERNATIVE: Ask your friends these questions and compare notes on your answers.

QUESTIONS:

1. An ice cream shop is naming a new flavor of ice cream after you. What does it taste like and why?

2. Aliens have landed on Earth, and they want you to explain what love is to them. What do you say?

3. A mad scientist is turning you into a plant. Which one would you would prefer to be and why?

4. You've discovered the secret to traveling back in time, but someone in the past has to trade places with you. Who do you want living your life for you while you're gone?

5. You have the power to erase ten minutes of time. When would you use it and why?

6. You've discovered you have a new superpower! What is it? How would you use it?

7. You've been asked to describe your favorite color to someone who has been blind since birth. What do you tell them?

8. You've been given a million dollars, but you can't keep any of it, you can't buy anything for yourself with it, and you can't give it to your friends or family. What do you do with it?

9. You have the opportunity to visit yourself as a child, but you can only tell yourself one fact about your life or one piece of advice. What would it be?

10. You wake up naked in a hardware store. What do you use for clothes? And how do you explain your predicament?

11. You realize you're dreaming and can control what's happening in your dream. What do you do?

12. You discover a door to a secret room in your house. What's in it?

13. If you could have a dinner with three fictional characters from different sources, who would they be and why?

14. You've been asked to describe your favorite song to someone who has been deaf since birth. What do you tell them?

15. You pass a tree that has money hanging from it. What do you do?*

So, is it bigger than a bread box?

MONEY DOES GROW ON TREES

*Writer Amy Krouse Rosenthal actually did leave real money hanging from a tree and documented what happened! Watch the results and see the other inspiring creative projects Amy has done, including *The Beckoning of Lovely*, on her site:

www.whoisamy.com

BETH BROWN is an author who has created her own yearlong creative project she calls Trinket a Day.

5 EASY WAYS TO STOP TALKING AND START DOING

I once organized a networking group for writers where folks could get together and offer support to newcomers to the field. While there were a handful of published authors among the group, the majority were not. I found out that most of them enjoyed having the dream of being a writer but never got any closer to that dream.

Excuses were plenty, mind you. "I just don't have enough time to write that novel right now" or "I had to work late so I didn't get that story started this week" or "My kids were loud so I figured I'd just start this weekend."

Lots of these folks floundered for months, even years, before getting the first words written. You know what they had to say after that? "Why didn't I start last week/month/year/decade?"

Here are five simple things you can do now (not tomorrow!) to get you moving:

1. Work first thing in the morning.
No matter what your medium, put in your creative effort first thing in the morning. This works because you're unlikely to get bogged down with the mental clutter of daily life before you put in your YOU time.

2. Work for ten to fifteen minutes only.

Yes, another mental trick! There is far less to lose when you're only dedicating yourself to a small bite of time, and you're much more likely to commit if the work is quick and easy.

3. Break down large goals into smaller ones.

Want to write a book? Make your goal today to write a paragraph. Yes, start that small and gradually work yourself up to loftier achievements like pages and chapters. You will build up a momentum of success.

4. Reward yourself for meeting your goals.

Finished that paragraph? Have a chocolate. Finished that page? Go play at the playground. Humans thrive on praise, even when it only comes from yourself!

5. Make yourself accountable to someone else.

You may not have a boss or an editor breathing down your neck, but fear (of embarrassment) can be a great motivator. Have a trusted friend agree to pester you about your progress. For an added bonus, have them hold a twenty-dollar bill hostage until you deliver the creative goods you promised.

I've done every single one of these things with my "Make Something Everyday" project and can attest to their performance!

Beth Brown is an author, artist, and freelance curmudgeon from Richmond, Virginia. She shares her adventures with her husband, daughter, son, and menagerie of rescued animals.

www.beth-brown.com
www.trinketaday.com

CREATIVE ADVICE

15

DADA POETRY

The early twentieth-century art movement known as Dada was all about the rejection of the normal way of doing things. The international members of the group used a variety of creative tools (like collage, performance, and music) to create work that jarred people out of their normal life experiences.

Taking a cue from the Dadaists, your task is to create a nonsense poem using only found words. This will get you thinking about the difference between the physical forms of words and the meanings we assign them. As you begin to see that these things are arbitrary, what else in your world will you start to look at differently?

HOW TO DO IT:

1. Find one or more newspapers, magazines, or books that you don't mind altering.

2. Cut out words that look interesting to you. Don't worry about what they mean. You can even cut the words up into parts.

3. After you've amassed at least twenty, pick words randomly and put them in lines until you've used them up. Remember, the goal is not to make something that makes sense.

4. Rearrange the pieces if you feel like some words would sound better together.

5. Read the resulting poem out loud.

6. Attach your favorite parts to the space provided on the next page so that you can revisit them later.

Document your poetry here . . .

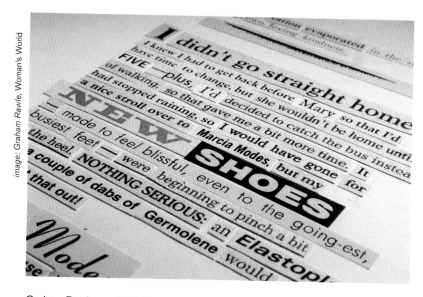

image: Graham Rawle, Woman's World

Graham Rawle created his novel *Woman's World* by first writing it and then replacing every word with ones he cut out from 1960s women's magazines.

Document your poetry here . . .

BONUS: Invite some friends over to hear a reading of your creation. Read dramatically and with inflection as if this were a completely sensible poem.

SAY WHAT?

Artist Hugo Ball (1886-1927) was a founding member of the Dada movement. His poem "Karawane," from 1916, is a classic example of Dada art. Made up entirely of nonsense words, the poem was read aloud by Ball at the Cabaret Voltaire in Zurich, Switzerland, while wearing a cardboard costume.

KARAWANE

jolifanto bambla ô falli bambla
grossiga m'pfa habla horem
égiga goramen
higo bloiko russula huju
hollaka hollala
anlogo bung
blago bung
blago bung
bosso fataka
ü üü ü
schampa wulla wussa ólobo
hej tatta gôrem
eschige zunbada
wulubu ssubudu uluw ssubudu
tumba ba- umf
kusagauma
ba - umf

(1917)
Hugo Ball
53

poem: Hugo Ball, "Karawane," in Dada-Almanach, edited by Richard Huelsenbeck (Berlin: Erich Reiss Verlag, 1920), p. 53. From a copy in the International Dada Archive, Special Collections, University of Iowa Libraries.

INSPIRATION

16

DRAW WITH YOUR EYES

SKILLS

1₀
MINUTE
PROJECTS

There's so much inspiration in the world around us, we just have to keep our eyes open. But often once we've seen something that inspires us, we switch our eyes back off. This is an exercise in staying focused on what we see and not what we think.

HOW TO DO IT:

1. Choose a marking tool of your choice (marker, pen, pencil, etc.).
2. Choose a subject in your immediate vicinity.
3. Spend the next ten minutes drawing exactly what you see without looking at your page (use the space provided or your own paper). Follow the contours of what is really in front of you with your eyes and move your tool accordingly. This isn't about reproducing something perfectly, so no peeking 'til you're done!

ALTERNATIVE: Don't lift your tool for the entire time you're working so that the image is made with one continuous line. This technique is called blind contour drawing.

76

Get drawing . . .

PHOTO MASH-UP

One way to change your perspective is to take two incongruous things and put them together. DJs do this in a musical technique called mash-ups where two unrelated songs are merged into one new song, usually with the music from one and the vocals from the other. To do this visually, most people would employ Photoshop® or other digital tools, but this is an exercise you can do with only the most basic of tools.

HOW TO DO IT:
1. Find two images that are relatively the same size and that you don't mind altering. These can be old photographs or pictures from magazines, books, etc.
2. Cut the images into thin slices. One image should be cut horizontally and one cut vertically.
3. Interweave the two images so that you maintain the original relationships of the slices.

ALTERNATIVE: Try cutting one of the two images in uneven or even curvy slices and see how that changes the results. Or try weaving that is not consistent (two over, one under; one over, two under; etc.).

What offspring did your unusual pairings produce?

SUPER SIZED

Philosopher Marshall McLuhan famously said "the medium is the message," but if you're stuck, the message may be that you need a new medium! In this exercise, you're going to spend a bit of time working at a different scale and on a different surface so that your ideas are freed of the constraints of the normal media you work with.

HOW TO DO IT:

1. Find a piece of chalk or charcoal. It doesn't specifically have to be sidewalk chalk. It's always better to work with material you have at hand.

2. Head outside to the nearest sidewalk. If the weather won't allow you to work outside, a garage or other indoor space where the floor is meant to get dirty will work too.

3. Spend ten minutes continuing whatever your current project happens to be, but at the scale and angle that is required by this new surface and tool. This may involve some creative problem solving if your project isn't just writing or drawing!

4. Use the space provided to document what you did, how you felt, and how other people responded. Be sure to take a picture or two as well since this should be a purely temporary thing you've created.

What messages did your medium give you?

ALTERNATIVE: Buy several yards of the largest paper you can find on a roll at an art or craft store and use it as your surface. Try using it on both the floor and hanging it on the wall and see how the different locations affect you.

**10
MINUTE
PROJECTS**

BEAUTIFUL BODY

Artists in the Surrealist movement of the early twentieth century made up a creative game that involved group collaboration called Exquisite Corpse. They would take turns adding images or words on a folded page so that they could not see what came before or only had just enough to continue. The end results were surprising and funny and allowed for unusual connections that might not normally have been made. This project gives you a chance to get the benefits of random play and spending time being creative with others.

HOW TO DO IT:

1. Find one or more people to work with you on this.
2. Each person, including you, should fold a piece of paper into quarters as shown.
3. Add the words "head," "torso," "legs," and "feet" in order, one on each section.
4. Start at the bottom or top and draw a head or feet of your choice. Extend the lines that reach the fold just slightly over it so that the next person has a starting place to work from.
5. Fold the paper so that your work can't be seen by the next person.
6. Pass the pieces back and forth or around in a circle until all spaces have been used up and then reveal the end results to the group.

Document the results of your Doctor Frankenstein experience here . . .

ALTERNATIVE: For a really surreal result, leave off the names of the parts of the body and let people draw whatever they want as long as it connects.

BARRY LOUIS POLISAR has been making music for more than thirty years. The ultimate irony in his career came in 2007 when film director Jason Reitman was searching iTunes for a song and typed in the wrong title. He discovered Barry's song "All I Want Is You" from 1977 and ended up using it in the opening credits of his film *Juno*. The music soundtrack sold over a million copies worldwide and won a Grammy Award.

JUMP IN AND GET DIRTY

photo: Michael G. Ste

I have never been the kind of writer who locks himself in a room and doesn't emerge until he has created something. I think the pressure to create on demand can lead to sloppy and inconsequential work. I do think it's important to observe and listen to the things around me—and to be unafraid of jumping in.

I've thrown my heart and soul into countless writing and music projects over the years—but also into other kinds of creative projects as well. I've tackled stream cleanups and renovated old houses. It's sometimes overwhelming to think about large projects, but once I get started, it always goes faster—and is more fun—than I expect. This is how I approach every creative project; I take that first step and never look back. To an outside observer, taking time away from writing songs to wrestle two hundred junked tires out of a wooded ravine might seem like walking away from creativity . . . but to me, it's all one in the same.

> ## *"This is how I approach every creative project; I take that first step and never look back."*

Part of the creative process is being able to recognize the gifts you are handed. I began writing and singing for children after a teacher saw me with my guitar and asked me if I would come to her school and perform for her students. I could have come up with a number of reasons to decline the invitation since I was still learning, but I didn't. At that very first school concert, I heard a teacher yelling at her students and copied down what she said. That night I wrote a song called "I've Got a Teacher, She's So Mean." Within months, teachers began calling to see if I could come to their school to sing the song.

The feedback inspired me to write even more songs. Eventually, I began thinking about recording an album. I never expected it would be the start of a writing career that would last for three and a half decades.

Barry Louis Polisar has traveled throughout the United States and Europe, performing in art centers, schools, and libraries. He has performed at the Kennedy Center for the Performing Arts, the Smithsonian, and the White House. A five-time Parents' Choice Award Winner, Barry has written songs for Sesame Street *and* The Weekly Reader *and starred in an Emmy-Award winning television show for children. He has written and published over a dozen books, and his songs have been recorded by people throughout the world.*

www.BarryLou.com

CREATIVE ADVICE

ON THE MOVE

Very often our creative time is spent sitting in one spot for hours on end. While this may be necessary, it's definitely not healthy and certainly not inspiring. The simple act of getting up and moving around can immediately put your brain into a different gear. This exercise just asks you to add a bit of movement to your work.

HOW TO DO IT:

1. Pick out some music that gets you moving and put it on.

2. Spend the next ten minutes working on one of your usual creative activities or in the space provided, but you have to be standing up and moving the entire time. This could be isolated movement or your entire body.

ALTERNATIVE: If you don't have a specific project to work on, just draw or paint using your body's movements to create the gestures on the page.

What happened when you got moving?

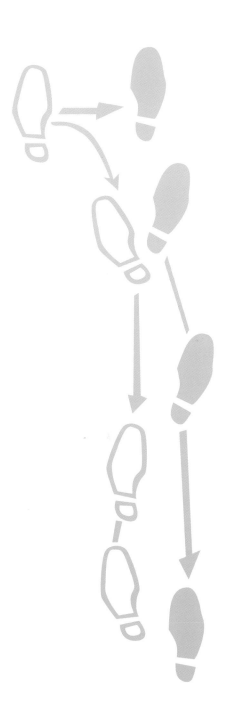

21

1❂ MINUTE PROJECTS

ACT NATURALLY

Unless your job specifically involves working outside, you're probably spending most of your creative time indoors. Even if you have a creative workspace, there's still no replacing the great outdoors when it comes to inspiration. Nature's solutions to problems are generally simple, elegant, and direct. If your brain is making things too complicated, this is a task for you.

HOW TO DO IT:

1. Head outside for at least ten minutes.
2. Spend your time observing the natural world around you. See what elements of the work that you already do are represented in the things you observe. Can you find lines similar to those you draw? Or forms similar to the tools you use? Can you see interactions that remind you of the way your own work functions? Or do you see things that you could apply to your working methods to improve them?
3. Note your findings in the space provided.

What did you discover outside?

ASK NATURE!

Many great inventions were created by observing nature. The hooks and eyes of Velcro® fasteners were inspired by the way burrs stick to dog fur. The material used for recent competition swimsuits is based on tiny details of shark's skin. The nosecone of Japan's bullet train is based on the beak of the kingfisher, which reduces sound and improves speed and energy efficiency!

For more inspiring stories of new nature-inspired design, check out:

www.AskNature.org

INSPIRATION

REWIND

Sometimes the best way to move forward is to spend some time going backward. It may sound counterintuitive but, if you find you've hit a wall that you can't push your way through, there's probably a path around it that you can only find by heading back up the path for a bit. This exercise asks you to spend some time going in the wrong direction.

HOW TO DO IT:

1. Take whatever project you are currently working on and spend the next ten minutes doing the opposite of what you've been doing. Be creative with how this could be done. Instead of cutting apart, start gluing together; instead of drawing, start erasing, etc.

2. Document what happened and what thoughts came to you while doing this. Any insights into your working process? Any alternate paths forward become visible?

10 MINUTE PROJECTS

BONUS: What would an entirely inverse project look like? What if you started a project where you would normally end it? What assumptions are you making about the order of your personal process? Do things have to always happen in the order you always do them? The solution will be unique to you; it could just be a quick experiment or something you do over the course of an entire day or more!

CHANGE THE RULES

photo: Gray West

Back in 2009, I was asked to do a piece for someone's book about "geek crafts," a genre that could include any craft but whose themes were sci-fi, video game, and cult show/movie oriented. I like all that stuff, but I'm not deeply familiar with it. The author, Susan Beal, sent me a list of possible shows and games, and I found myself at a loss. I didn't have cable during the years of *Buffy the Vampire Slayer* and *Firefly* and even missed *The X-Files*. I've never been a big gamer so Super Mario Brothers was out.

I knew I needed a close connection to the project or it wouldn't turn out well. If I picked something I had only a passing acquaintance with, I'd end up phoning it in and being unhappy with the result.

For inspiration, I spent a Saturday watching my favorite sci-fi movies. Popcorn in hand, I watched *Aliens*, *It Came from Outer Space*, *Invasion of the Body Snatchers*, *War of the Worlds*, and, finally, *The Day the Earth Stood Still* (my all-time favorite). And then it hit me. If I couldn't get excited about anything on the list, I could just ask to change the rules. Ten minutes later, I was emailing Susan to ask if I could do something with Gort, the robot from *The Day the Earth Stood Still*. She said yes, and I was off and running.

My second problem was the actual project. Armed only with my idea, I went to the studio and started digging around. I found an old toolbox that reminded me of the cool old lunchboxes with TV shows and movies on them. I decided to emblazon Gort, in all his laser-shooting glory, on it. Of course, I didn't want to just paint him on there. I wanted it to be different, special. A stack of design magazines had been languishing in a corner, and even though I'd never tried it, I decided to do up the box with paper mosaic.

Eighty hours later, my studio littered with hundreds of confettti-like scraps of paper and little dried puddles of Mod Podge, I was done. I was happy. The author was happy. The next day, it appeared on Boing Boing, where it was purchased by a famous Hollywood director. Before it was shipped off to him, it ended up being used for the cover shot of the book, *World of Geekcraft*.

Hard beginning. Super happy ending!

"And then it hit me. If I couldn't get excited about anything on the list, I could just ask to change the rules."

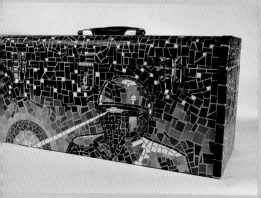

photo: Paul Overton

Paul Overton *is a prolific blogger, maker, writer, and ukulele player living in Durham, North Carolina, with four dogs, two co-conspirators, and a lawn that makes his neighbors want to call the authorities. He delights in the unusual and can often be found in his tiny studio next to the record shop, whipping up some sort of self-indulgent nonsense for his own amusement.*

www.DudeCraft.com
www.EveryDayIsAwesome.com

YOUR BODY, YOURSELF

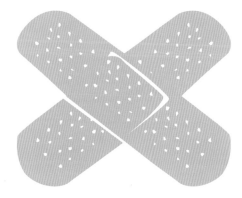

10 MINUTE PROJECTS

You are carrying around a world of ideas with you all the time. You've collected experiences over the course of your life that have had a physical impact on your body. So instead of looking in your head for inspiration, this task asks you to look in a mirror.

HOW TO DO IT:

1. Take a few moments to think about the various marks you've collected on your body throughout your life, both intentional (like tattoos and piercings) and unintentional (like surgery scars, stretch marks, and bruises). Use the space at right to catalog them.

2. Choose one and take the next ten minutes to create something inspired by it. Think about it in context of the work you're doing or just use this as a way to fire up your creative engine. This could be a short story based on the reason for a scar, a visual piece using a photo of a tattoo as the base, or even something that hangs from or accentuates a piercing hole. Don't limit yourself to your usual skill-set; let the subject matter drive this project.

My Body Catalog:

**What part of your body was your inspiration?
And what did it inspire you to do?**

24

EPITAPH

The term *memento mori* ("reminder of death") dates back to the Middle Ages. But the idea that seeing things that make you think about your death will help you remember to live life fully has probably been around for as long as humans have existed. This task is not meant to be depressing; rather it's a chance to put things in perspective. Plus the ability to condense big ideas into small spaces is a very useful skill to develop. If you're taking your work a bit too seriously, this is for you.

HOW TO DO IT:
  1. Spend a few minutes thinking about how you would want to be remembered when you die.
  2. Write an epitaph for yourself on one of the tombstones provided that quickly sums up what you want the world to remember about you.
  3. Use the additional tombstones for alternate epitaphs that you come up with when you need another moment to appreciate your life now.

Write in peace . . .

BONUS: Imagine that you've lived to age 100. Write a short obituary for yourself featuring some details of your accomplishments that take place between now and then.

30 MINUTE PROJECTS

FIND YOUR DESK MUSE

25

WHERE

SKILLS

30 MINUTE PROJECTS

Artist Terry Border (see page 151) creates remarkable characters full of emotion with everyday objects and a bit of wire. He's mastered the art of creating something new out of the things most people don't think about twice in their daily lives. Once you start thinking of things around you as full of creative potential, it's hard to stop! This is your chance to give Terry's method a try and create a little inspiring character for your workspace.

HOW TO DO IT:

1. Gather together some objects in your workspace that you don't mind sacrificing for creativity. This is a good chance to use up some materials that have been sitting around for a while.

2. Spend a few moments finding the character potential in the items and choose which one(s) to work with.

3. Use paperclips or thin-gauge wire if you have any (picture-hanging wire and floral wire will work too) to add appendages and other details to your objects. Keep in mind that the end result can be human, animal, or even a fantastical creature of your own creation. Look at Terry's work for inspiration on how very simple shapes can be used for most details.

4. Try to make it so that the figure can stand up on its own. Maybe it will need a prop (like a walking stick made from a pencil) to help it out.

BONUS: Create a short story about your character.

Document your process and results here . . .

How do people react to your new muse?

photo: Joel Saget, AFP, Getty Images

A CIRCUS OF WIRE

Check out the wonderfully whimsical work of artist
Alexander Calder (1898–1976), who built an entire
interactive circus from wire and found objects!

See examples of Calder's work
on his foundation's website:
www.calder.org

26

MEAL EMOTIONS

Mealtimes are one of my favorite times for creative inspiration. Generally you're away from your usual environment and you've got unusual materials right in front of you. This project was developed with a group of my fellow designers when we met up for lunch and wanted to do something other than just talk about the usual work woes.

HOW TO DO IT:

1. Clip out the emotions provided in the back of the book on pages 231–235 or write them on slips of paper and put them in a small bag. Keep them in your pocket, purse, or backpack so you have them when the moment is right.

2. After you eat, choose one of the emotions out of the bag without looking.

3. Using only leftover food and other items on the table, create a face that shows the emotion.

4. Take a photo so you can share the results, since this will be a purely temporary creation.

What faces did you make?

OPTION: Invite a group to do this project with you. It's fun to see how different people work with similar materials. Keep the emotion secret and then take turns guessing what each face represents!

ALTERNATIVE: Instead of emotions, write out a list of animals or objects and use them instead.

BONUS: If you do this at a restaurant, consider leaving the face as a surprise for the server. If you've made a big mess in the process, definitely clean up as much as you can and leave a nice tip!

Excited

The leftovers from my nachos became the source material when my friends and I gave this project a try for the first time. Other faces that day included "bemused" made with croutons and parsley and "surprised" made with pizza crust and a lemon wedge!

photo: Chris Moore

SLASH COLEMAN is a professional storyteller who performs internationally.

ALTER EGOS

When I suddenly found myself with a venue that not only wanted to play hardball, but didn't have my best interests at heart, I didn't have the luxury of leaning back in my chair and saying to an officemate, "Here, why don't you handle this one?" With an expensive gig at stake, I did what every thoughtful, money-strapped, creative-minded artist has the ability to do. I created a make-believe personal assistant named Agnew Hamilton.

Agnew secured his own email address with the name "agent" in it and emailed back something to the venue along the following lines: "Due to the success of my client's production and the volume of emails that my client is now receiving, I have been hired on as the personal assistant to negotiate the terms of all future performance contracts." Agnew laid down a minimum price per performance, and the terms included travel and board.

Bam! Whereas the theater department had dragged its feet with contacting me before, Agnew received a response within a day. But there was more! The department was attempting to locate a mysterious funding source that they had previously overlooked.

"I didn't have the luxury of leaning back in my chair and saying to an officemate, 'Here, why don't you handle this one?'"

Since then, Agnew's been working off and on when I need him, and I have to tell you people respond very differently to him than they do to me. He has a certain arrogance that I don't, and he looks negotiations, contracts, and money talk squarely in the eyes.

Although I created Agnew partly out of necessity and partly as a joke, playing the role of this imaginary personal assistant through the years has boosted my self-esteem and my self-confidence and taken my creativity to a whole new level.

Since then, I've added an entire posse of imaginary people to keep me creatively inspired. Besides Agnew, I also have an imaginary agent, an imaginary business partner, and an imaginary Yenta (matchmaker). Some maintain their own Facebook page, others maintain a blog or website, and one even maintains a dating profile.

When I speak through my imaginary characters, it allows me to express myself without fear of judgment (either from my self-censor or from others). In addition, there's just something appealing about the distance of using an alter ego to express myself that feels freeing—like I'm six again and I'm sitting on the floor doodling in my sketchpad, coloring outside the lines, making the grass blue and the sky green.

With an eccentric sculptor as a father, a dancer at the Moulin Rouge as a grandfather, and a watercolorist as a grandmother, **Slash Coleman** *is a professional storyteller who is best known for his award-winning PBS special,* The Neon Man and Me. *His marketing classes for artists were recently featured on the NPR series* How Artists Make Money.

www.slashcoleman.com

CREATIVE ADVICE

VIDEOPHONE

WHERE

SKILLS

Telephone is a classic party game that goes by a variety of names such as Grapevine, Gossip, Broken Telephone, and Whisper Down the Lane. In a circle of people, one person whispers a phrase in the ear of the person next to them and that person whispers the same message to the next person along. Typically the message gets back to the original person completely garbled and hilarity ensues. This project is a creative variation I was taught by some friends of mine. The best part is that getting the wrong answer is much more entertaining than getting it right.

HOW TO DO IT:

1. Gather together a group of five or more people. This project is especially good with large groups, but it takes more time the more people that are included.
2. Each person starts with a small stack of blank paper. For large groups, there should be at least as many pieces of paper as there are people participating.
3. Each person writes a short, common phrase on their top sheet of paper (i.e., "No Shirt, No Shoes, No Service," "Faster than a speeding bullet!," etc.).

4. Everyone then passes their stack of paper to the person to their right.

5. After reading the phrase written on the paper you've just been given, shift it to the bottom of the pile and then draw an image that portrays the phrase without any words.

6. The stacks of paper are again handed to the right, and once again the top sheet is shifted to the bottom after you look at it.

7. This time write out the phrase that you think is represented by the drawing you've been given. While you can go for accuracy and try to figure out the phrase, it's way more fun to take the drawing as literally as possible.

8. Continue passing the stacks—alternating between drawing and writing—until you've gone through at least one revolution of the group or until you've run out of paper.

9. When you stop, share the top image or phrase with the group and then work your way backward until you get to the original seed.

ALTERNATIVE: This could be done with three to four people by starting with a drawing rather than a phrase, making it that much harder to figure out what the message is supposed to be.

Document how your messages got transmitted:

PSYCHO-GEOGRAPHY

Our brains get into ruts we create by following the same paths over and over. This project is a chance to rewrite these pathways. Even just taking a different route home from being out and about can cause you to think differently. Taking a cue from the Situationists (page 117), here's your chance to chart a new course.

HOW TO DO IT:
1. Choose one of the "maps" provided or take some extra time to make one of your own in the same spirit.
2. Step out the door and take a walk using the map. The map won't literally relate to your surroundings; the point is to do your best to stick to it, even if that means walking in some unusual places or ways.
3. Record your experiences along the way in the spaces provided.

BONUS: Invite others to join you on your trip. Or even create and swap maps with your friends and document the results.

ALTERNATIVE: Use the map to get you to a familiar destination or run an errand even if it takes you far out of the way.

Where did your map take you?

What happened along the way?

REJECT THE RUT

The Situationists, who coined the term psychogeography, were a group of artist activists in the 1950s and 1960s in France who wanted to encourage people to live fuller lives by rejecting the spectacle of modern consumer culture. To that end they created situations (using graffiti, pranks, and other tools) that would cause people to break out of their normal life experiences. One of their areas of focus was rethinking how people interact with the urban environment, particularly as pedestrians. They used altered maps to help people rediscover the city in unexpected ways.

Find out more about the Situationists here:

www.nothingness.org/SI

INSPIRATION

CENSORED POETRY

Since too many options can be overwhelming, giving yourself a limited amount of material to work with is a great way to narrow your focus and get you back to being creative. Why write new words when we're swimming in them already? You don't have to be a poet or writer to take advantage of this technique. The key is having fun and learning to see new ways to work with materials you handle every day.

HOW TO DO IT:

1. Choose a page of a newspaper, magazine, book, or other document that has plenty of words on it that you don't mind altering.

2. Scan it for words that fit together to make a new message that's unrelated to the content. You can use a current project as the subject matter or just let the words direct you.

3. Circle or draw boxes around the words you have selected.

4. Using a marker or paint, cover over the rest of the words on the page. This can be just a big solid shape or you can connect the boxes in a creative way (i.e., with arrows pointing from one to the next, or with decorative frames, or with abstract shapes, etc.).

ALTERNATIVE: Work as a group. Each person starts with their own paper and chooses one word or phrase and then passes it to the next person who selects the next word or phrase. Keep doing this until you get your original paper back. Then take turns reading the results.

Document your censored poetry experiments here . . .

What materials worked best?

What were your favorite poems?

AUSTIN KLEON'S NEWSPAPER BLACKOUT POEMS

This project was inspired by the work of Austin Kleon. Austin is a writer and artist who started making his own poetry out of newspapers while riding back and forth to work on the bus. Dubbed **Newspaper Blackout Poems** his work has since been collected into a book.

image: Austin Kleon

forget about

trying to

speak

The image is

the

travelogue

Check out more of Austin's poems and even share your own creations here:

NewspaperBlackout.com

WHERE

SKILLS

FOREIGN TRAVEL

"One of my most frequent sources of inspiration is a newly occupied hotel room. I find it easy to work in a place far away from the studio, where thoughts about the implementation of an idea don't come to mind immediately but I can dream a bit more freely."

—Stefan Sagmeister

As I collected interviews for this book, time and again the point was made that getting out of your environment is one of the best ways to get the creative process rolling. And some of the best new environments are found when you travel away from home. Obviously that's not something you can do the moment you need some inspiration, so here's a chance to get a taste of foreign travel near home.

HOW TO DO IT:

1. See if your area has any shops that specialize in foods from another country. I don't live in a big city, and yet there are Asian, Indian, and Hispanic specialty stores within a few miles. If you can't find one, go to a large grocery store with a foreign foods aisle.

2. Head to the store and imagine that you're actually in the country where the items are from.

3. Spend your time looking at the differences in packaging from what you're familiar with, trying to decipher words you don't know and imagining how items you don't recognize might be used.

4. Document your travels in the space provided.

How was your trip?

BONUS: While it's not required, buying one or two small items to bring back with you is not only polite, but it will carry the experience back to your workspace. If it's edible, you can try it for an unusual taste experience, or you can use what you got as art material!

LEAH LAMB is a writer, producer, actor, playwright, and lifelong activist.

GET ON THE DANCE FLOOR AND MOVE

photo: Leah Lamb

Step 1: Never leave the house without a pen and mini notebook. We all have ideas. It's what we do with those ideas that distinguishes the "professional creatives" from all of the other talented people. When new ideas arrive, greet them as wanted guests, setting up a room for them so they can flourish (a.k.a. "writing the ideas down").

Step 2: Look at the world as if it is there for the sole purpose of inspiring your creative endeavor. I've found metaphors in the turned-out back pocket of the guy walking his dog, a memory in the waving shadow of a plant bursting through the sidewalk, and a key to a character's heart inside my cat's snore.

Step 3: Take your dreams seriously. They are the unconscious unwinding and reorganizing of the details of your life, making sense of things in ways your conscious cannot. Some of the most beloved and complex stories were born in dreams.

Step 4: Cheat the warm-up period. I begin each new story by finding its musical soundtrack. These songs hold the rhythm, the feeling, and the emotional content of what I want to create. Every time I write, I put on my headphones and am transported inside the world of the story.

> **"It's a dance with the creative, and you have to be willing to get on the dance floor and move when the music calls to you."**

Step 5: Trust. Trust. Trust. Practice. Practice. Practice.

Be willing to blur your eyes, stop thinking, and ride the idea that drops in, even if it only takes you for a short ride. It's like exercise; you're always preparing for the big wave so that when it comes you will have the skill to ride it. Trust comes with practice. Maybe your practice happens once a week or maybe ten minutes a day.

Step 6: Kill writer's block.

When you're in a rut, there is nothing like going for a walk or a run, or putting the story in a drawer and letting it rest for a bit, trusting that this act is an active step toward making space for the answers to filter in.

Step 7: Don't try to be good.

I had some amazing teachers early on who gave me permission to take risks and not be attached in the creative process. When you think about being good, you are no longer engaged in the process. Come to your creativity as you would a lover: ready, eager, present and in the moment, without a plan on how to experience the pleasure. It's a dance with the creative, and you have to be willing to get on the dance floor and move when the music calls to you. In the meantime, practice your dance steps.

Leah Lamb worked as a wilderness guide for seven years and tortured herself with a masters degree in social work, after which she became the founding online producer for Current.com's green channel. She is completing her first novel, and her random thoughts about the environment can be found on The Huffington Post, Discovery's Planet Green, NatGeo News Watch, and TreeHugger.

www.LeahLamb.com

WHERE

SKILLS

PHANTOM LIMB

It's often said that when people lose the use of one of their senses, the others will get better to compensate. Of course this happens over time, and at first I'm sure the world is a disorienting place. While that can be unpleasant if you have a permanent loss and are trying to go about your normal life, it can be an inspiring temporary experience for creativity.

HOW TO DO IT:

1. Take your dominant arm (i.e., the one with the hand you normally write with) and secure it to your side by sticking it in your waistband, or using a belt, tape, or string to loosely tie it to your side. This is just meant as a reminder so you won't accidentally use it, but it should still be easy for you to use your arm in an emergency situation.

2. Spend the next thirty minutes going about whatever you were doing previously.

3. In the space provided, note your experiences. What was different? What was the same? How could you apply this experience in the future?

Did you miss your limb?

How were things different without it?

BONUS: Extend the time to an hour, a day, or more!

ALTERNATIVE: Try not using a leg or even both arms if you need a greater challenge.

TIED TOGETHER

Performance artists Linda Montano and Tehching Hsieh took this idea to the extreme when they spent a year (July 1983 to July 1984) tied together by the waist with an eight-foot rope! And they didn't touch each other this entire time. Can you imagine what they learned about themselves in the process?

See more about the artists on their respective sites:

Linda Montano
www.lindamontano.com

Techhing Hsieh
www.one-year-performance.com

INSPIRATION

MAD SCIENTIST

According to my friend and fellow artist Matthew Lively (see page 48), creativity is a lot more like science than people realize. It's all about experimenting and doing things over and over until you get the results you want. He uses the example of the popular cleaning product Formula 409®, whose name actually comes from the fact that it was the 409th attempt by the scientists who created it!

This project is a chance to just do some experimenting of your own that's not about the end results but the process itself. You never know what the results will bring.

HOW TO DO IT:
1. Gather together materials that you typically use.
2. Start picking out pairs of items you would never usually put together (i.e., a pencil and water).
3. Spend the next thirty minutes trying out these combinations.
4. Use the space provided to document the results of your experiments. What surprised you? Did you discover any new techniques that you might want to use again?

Document your experiments here . . .

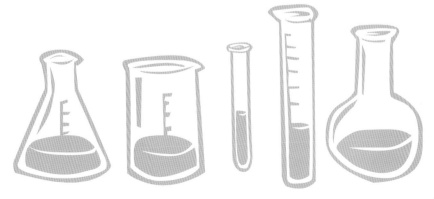

What materials did you use?
What were the results of your experiments?

BONUS: Create a grid with all of the items listed across the top and down the side. Then go through the matrix of trying all possible combinations.

ALTERNATIVE: Go to an art or office supply store, buy a few materials you've never tried before, and replace some of the things you normally work with.

FAILED EXPERIMENTS
OR UNEXPECTED INVENTIONS?

Sometimes experiments that seem to have failed just need a new perspective put on them:

Silly Putty® was invented in 1943 by an engineer named James Wright, who was looking for a way to create synthetic rubber, but no one knew what to do with this weird bouncy stuff. It didn't become a toy until 1949 when it was discovered by Ruth Fallgatter, a toy store owner in Connecticut.

Post-it® notes came about when Dr. Spencer Silver created an adhesive that didn't stick very well. It was only six years later that 3M coworker Art Fry came up with the idea to use it for a bookmark that wouldn't slide out of a book!

INSPIRATION

MARK-MAKING LIBRARY

Sometimes the limits we experience come from the tools we use. The assumption that there is one right way to use things can get you in the habit of allowing them to control you, rather than the other way around. This project is a chance to explore and play with the tools you use for creativity.

HOW TO DO IT:

1. Choose a pen, pencil, or marker that you use regularly.

2. Using the spaces provided, try making marks per the directions given.

3. Use the blank spaces to try additional ideas that you think of yourself.

4. Refer back to your mark library when you need a reminder of the range that is possible in a single tool.

ALTERNATIVE: Do this exercise with another tool you use for creativity. How would this translate with a pair of scissors, a paintbrush, a sewing machine, a piano?

Start building your library here . . .

Sideways . . .

Upside down . . .

With your teeth . . .

With your toes . . .

By moving the book instead of the tool . . .

With the crook of your arm . . .

With your knees . . .

By moving your whole body while holding it in your hand . . .

Between pinky and ring finger . . .

Add your own mark-making ideas here . . .

X MARKS THE SPOT

A lot of creativity is about translation. Sometimes you are just inspired by something you've seen and create something new based on it, or you are given a message and asked to interpret it for a client. Honing this skill can help you jump right into the process of translation when you might otherwise be stumped as to how to move forward.

HOW TO DO IT:
1. Choose a place that you know how to get to. It could be somewhere near or far.
2. Create a map to that place that does not use any words or traditional map symbols. Think about what things you tell people when you direct them to places verbally. What landmarks do you talk about? Consider what people might hear or smell along the way. Don't restrict yourself to drawing. Try using other materials or even work in three dimensions.
3. If you choose somewhere nearby, instead of just making your map from memory, go on a walk and use photography and/or found objects to help create it.

How do you get there?

BONUS: Have someone use the map and follow them on their journey and see where you end up.

ALTERNATIVE: Make an audio version of your map.

AUDIO TOURIST

Artist Janet Cardiff uses the medium of the audio tour for her art. Requiring you to don a set of headphones, her voice guides you through places like Central Park in New York City, where she has you walk at a specific pace while she tells you a fictional story about the area. They are surreal and engrossing experiences that transform your ideas about the space you're in.

Check out Janet's work for more inspiration:

www.cardiffmiller.com

INSPIRATION

CATHY GRIER a.k.a. NYC-SubwayGirl is a singer/songwriter/performer who can often be found playing music for free underneath New York City.

TOUGH LOVE

Here are my thoughts about how to keep fueling a creative life.

Keep a journal of ideas and inspirations. It provides great resource material when you are blocked.
I find journaling in the morning is a great way to awaken my creativity. I sometimes journal while listening to public radio. I often hear interesting stories that inspire creativity to riff on. In addition to being a great writing exercise, journaling provides an endless source of material to draw from when I'm creatively blocked.

Bookmark sites and stories that can inspire material.
On my computer I keep a bookmark folder in my browser of interesting people, stories, or places I have discovered. When I need a creative nudge, I frequently go to that list. However, it's important to be mindful of Internet distractions and the temptation to click off topic.

Schedule creative time. Daily!
It's easier to stay focused on my writing when I establish a routine, especially when I don't have a particular project I'm working on.

With tough love, I schedule my creative time or I can get lost in the art of multitasking self-promotion. To ensure I get the best results, I experimented to find the time of day when I am most productive and stick with that time.

Use performing as a means to stimulate creativity.
When I have an idea for a song or need a new arrangement, I work it out during a subway gig. The chaotic environment of commuters provides a rhythmic texture that's inspirational. It's a collaboration of creativity in movement. I love learning through this process what songs suddenly stand out and get attention.

Nothing is gained by stressing.
Believing in yourself doesn't save you from ever being creatively stuck. But it should help you get through those moments when they do come. I believe my life's work is wholly designed for creativity so when I'm blocked I have learned not to stress about it. I quickly try to do some mundane task until I feel I've distracted myself away from any potential negative or unproductive thoughts. Then I go back to my creativity. If that doesn't work, I take a walk, have a tea break, or listen to the radio with my journal in hand.

Cathy Gier is a DIY singer/songwriter/performer who writes about community, activism, and social change on her website. She performs in public spaces in a program called Music Under New York.

www.NYCSubwayGirl.com

CREATIVE ADVICE

"With tough love, I schedule my creative time or I can get lost in the art of multitasking self-promotion."

WHERE

SKILLS

30
MINUTE
PROJECTS

BOOK WORM

Books are constant sources of inspiration for me.
Even though there's a ton of information online, there's
still nothing quite like the experience of making a random
discovery in a book. This exercise gives you an excuse to
do just that.

HOW TO DO IT:

1. Head to a nearby library or bookstore. (Try to keep
travel time to a minimum.)
2. Choose one of the directions at right and use it to
find a book. Interpret them how you wish so that you
end up with some words to work with.
3. Document what you find in the space provided.
4. Continue working on your current project using the
words you found as your inspiration.

NOTE: If you want to do a quicker version of this project
and have a decent collection of books at your home
or workspace, you can do this there, but you will be
missing out on the additional benefit of getting out of your
environment. Try to at least do the full version once before
doing the home version.

DIRECTIONS

Shelf 3
Book 6
Page 42
Sentence 12

Shelf 1
Book 10
Page 100
Sentence 3

Shelf 5
Book 2
Page 15
Sentence 1

Shelf 2
Book 15
Page 55
Sentence 8

Shelf 4
Book 8
Page 22
Sentence 5

What did you find? How will/did you use what you found?

BONUS: Create a quick short story or image inspired by the words you found.

ALTERNATIVE: Instead of looking for words, do the same process with books that are mainly filled with images and then use what you find for inspiration.

EAR SPY

There's a never-ending stream of words around us, whether they come from people talking on the phone or having conversations in person. Rather than tuning out these bits and pieces of sound, why not use them as inspiration? This is your chance to be a spy and collect some words surreptitiously from the people around you.

HOW TO DO IT:
1. Head out to a public area with plenty of people around.

2. Tune in to the conversations around you and write down small pieces that you hear in the space provided. Don't eavesdrop for too long; you're not trying to hear the entire story. Just get a piece that is interesting and move on. Be careful to make it look like you're just writing in your notebook and not actually listening to private stories.

3. Use what you hear as inspiration for your current project. Can you incorporate an actual line or an image it inspires into whatever you're doing?

What did you hear?

BONUS: Create a short story or image based on one or more of the lines.

How will/did you use what you heard?

OVERHEARD IN NEW YORK

For more inspiration check out the website Overheard in New York, which collects random humorous quips heard in the city that famously never sleeps and apparently is also always talking.

www.overheardinnewyork.com

IDEA HUNT

37

From TERRY BORDER, who began his Bent Objects series with the blog of the same name in 2006 (www.bentobjects.blogspot.com). His twisted images quickly found a worldwide audience, which led to a collection of his images in book form. Film critic Roger Ebert has since called him "brilliant," to which Terry replied, "Aww, shucks." His second book is *Bent Object of My Affection: The Twists and Turns of Love.*

 When I'm desperate for ideas, I go on the hunt for them. The best thing about this process is that not only is it usually productive, but I find that it's a lot of fun too.

HOW TO DO IT:
1. Go to the library or bookstore.
"I go to the library or bookstore, hopefully someplace attractive and maybe a place I haven't been before. I think that wakes up my brain a little. I think it's more alert in fresh surroundings, and for me looking at images on a computer screen has never led to anything successful. Something about having physical books [or] magazines in front of me makes a difference."

Terry Border. *photo: Terry Border*

30 MINUTE PROJECTS

2. Find a book that is chockfull of pictures of works by others. Maybe several of them. "I really like the yearly photographers' and illustrators' guides that feature hundreds of artists showing their work. There isn't a theme to those books, so turning each page is a total surprise in what I'll see next. I'm looking to load my head with as much imagery as I can. I'm not looking to steal ideas, but I find other artists' stuff very exciting, and I think of how I may be able to tackle their subject with a different spin and in my style."

3. Quickly sketch out any interesting ideas in the space provided. "Don't ever count on remembering any interesting thoughts when you are in the process of looking at so many images. Write or sketch something on a piece of paper so as to jog your memory later, and then forget about it and keep exciting your brain with new images."

Hamlet Was Nuts. *photo: Terry Border*

4. Get caffeinated. "Important—I do this all after drinking a good cup of coffee or strong tea. I'm sure it works without caffeine, but I'm pretty sure not as well. It's just another way of waking up part of my brain and getting it a bit excited. Excitement of some sort is a big plus."

5. Return and review. "Later, I look again at the ideas that I came up with and see what's usable. Most of them don't look quite as good as when I jotted them down, but there's usually something I can use. And I don't throw away the others because there have been so many times when I'll look back at a rejected idea and find a way to make it work."

6. Let it percolate. "My subconscious is a lot smarter than my awake self (even after a couple of cups of coffee). I sometimes find that during the next few days an idea will pop into my head when I'm doing something else, and it's very probable that it grew from a germ of an idea planted the day I tried to excite my brain with images. The mind keeps working, making connections— 'percolating' I like to call it. Those ideas are almost always my best."

Pretty Cupcakes. *photo: Terry Border*

What did you find on your hunt?
Sketch out your ideas here . . .

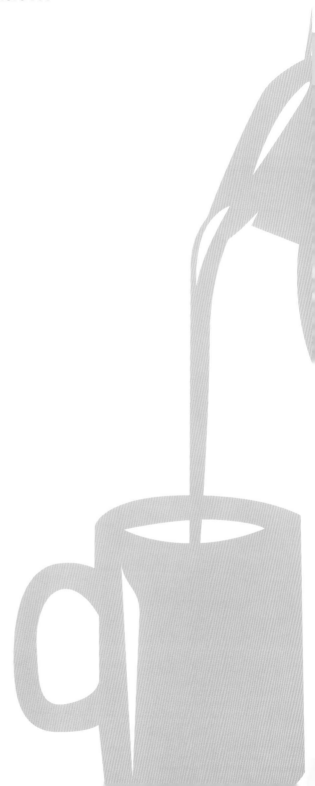

**LATER: Which of your ideas are usable?
How will you use them?**

ONE
HOUR
PROJECTS

CREATIVITY SHRINE

38

Having a large space dedicated to doing creative work in your home is wonderful but not always possible. However, having a small area that is dedicated to creative inspiration is a must. This can take a variety of forms and can even be portable. The key is having something that your eyes can glance at from time to time and that will remind you (even if it's just subliminally) about what gets your creative juices flowing.

ONE HOUR PROJECTS

HOW TO DO IT:

NOW:

1. Clear off a small section of a wall or a worktable to dedicate to your shrine. Try to make sure it's visible from wherever you normally spend your time doing creative work. If you prefer to make a portable one, start with a small box (shoeboxes or cigar boxes are a good size to work with).

2. Delineate the space by marking it off with tape, covering it with paper or paint, or even putting up a material like corkboard to use pins. Just make it clear that this is a distinctly separate space.

3. Fill the space with items you have already accumulated from travels or previous creative adventures. They can be all in a jumble or carefully arranged according to your own personal preferences.

4. Document the end result in the space provided.

LATER:
1. Keep your shrine in mind when you're out and about, and specifically pick up items (found or bought) to put in it when you return.
2. Replace items in your shrine periodically so that it doesn't just grow infinitely and take over the rest of your space!

ALTERNATIVE: Emptiness can be inspiring too. For some people a jumble of things is overwhelming instead of inspiring. So if your workspace is a total disaster area, perhaps your shrine is a square you keep perfectly empty, which will give your mind space to imagine what could be there.

My own creativity shrine takes up an entire corner of my office. I covered the wall with cork panels and pin-up items I've recently found, slowly rotating out old items as I find the new ones. The wall is where my eyes tend to go when I look away from my computer screen.

Document your shrine here . . .

Why did you choose the things you put in it?

SHERRY & JOHN PETERSIK run the popular do-it-yourself home improvement website Young House Love.

CHASING DOWN INSPIRATION

Since our blog revolves around taking on home improvement projects and transforming rooms on a serious budget, we're always looking for creative solutions—especially those that will save us money while adding function and form (which are both usually sorely lacking). We're no strangers to looking in a few odd places when it comes to getting ideas whenever our internal inspiration well runs dry. We truly believe that nothing in this world is new; solutions and ideas are just recycled and subconsciously revived and reinvented. And on occasion, just looking at things in a new way can solve all sorts of challenges.

For example, when we were looking for an affordable alternative to ordering custom cabinet doors for a doorless cabinet above our washer and dryer that we wanted to conceal, we walked through the area of our home improvement store where the blinds are located. Suddenly we realized that for about 5 percent of the cost of custom cabinetry, we could mount texture-rich bamboo blinds from the ceiling to conceal all the laundry clutter. And they could easily be raised and lowered for access to everything we needed. So if you're stuck, sometimes it just helps to walk around a store, park, café, or city street and really open your eyes while trying to imagine how you could reimagine something in a creative (and cost-effective) way.

As clichéd as it sounds, inspiration really is everywhere. We got a color scheme idea from fancy upscale soap packaging. Yes, we based an entire room on a paper soap wrapper with gorgeous tones of lime green, teal, navy, and white. The lesson? Even if something sounds like a crazy thing to use as a springboard for ideas, it can work. So if anything grabs you, we always recommend at least entertaining the thought before dismissing it as stupid.

Beyond relying on more traditional means of inspiration as well, we would just encourage you to do something. Anything. If you're paralyzed in fear that you'll mess up or make a mistake, you're no closer to accomplishing whatever you've set out to do. So remember that starting somewhere, doing something, and taking a chance is always going to get you closer to your goal than sitting on the sofa and waiting for inspiration to strike. Sometimes you have to chase it down instead.

*Painting, demo, and reno are all in a day's work for **John and Sherry Petersik**. In 2007, they bought an old seen-better-days brick ranch in Richmond, Virginia, and have been having fun with home improvement ever since. They even started a blog to document their adventures (and misadventures) called Young House Love, which gets 140,000 hits per day.*

www.YoungHouseLove.com

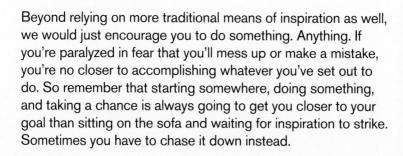

"As clichéd as it sounds, inspiration really is everywhere."

CREATIVE ADVICE

A YEAR IN AN HOUR

ONE
HOUR
PROJECTS

While I think everyone should take the time to do a yearlong, daily creative project, I realize that's not something everyone can just jump into, especially when they may need an immediate solution to a particular creative woe. This task is a way to get a taste of that 365 experience in a super-condensed time frame. Use this as an opportunity to get messy and have fun.

HOW TO DO IT:

1. Gather together plenty of random material to work with. I recommend digging in the recycling bin for this project. The more diverse the materials the better. It's also good to have plenty of cutting and marking tools along with items like staplers, string, tape, and glue sticks for attaching things as well.

2. Think of a simple shape you're comfortable making (star, heart, skull, etc.).

3. Try to create at least thirty versions of that shape in the next hour, using the materials you have collected. This is definitely about quantity over quality. Don't try for perfection. Just make it and move on to the next thing. If you find yourself stuck, move on to another material.

4. Document each item as you finish so that you can reuse parts of it as you move forward if need be!

5. When you're done, note in the space provided how you felt during this exercise and the things you learned about yourself in the process.

What did you make?

BONUS: If you finish all thirty things before the hour is up, see how many more things you can make!

Describe the experiences you had along the way . . .

I frequently lead creativity workshops where I do this exercise. People are usually overwhelmed at first, but once they let go of their need for perfection the ideas start flowing. I'm always impressed with the unusual solutions people come up with in the end.

ALTERNATIVE: Do this with a group of people. It makes for a very fun time and you may be surprised to see how others use the same materials in different ways. Plus, who says you can't work together to complete the assignment?

40

WHERE

SKILLS

**ONE
HOUR
PROJECTS**

GOING IN CIRCLES

This is a project that I frequently use when I give talks on generating creativity. I'm always impressed by how many ways there are to do this.

By the time I finished the first 100 days of my own 365-day project, I had gone through pretty much every idea and technique I'd ever experienced before. And that's when it got really good! Once you use up all the easy, obvious ideas that you carry around as your default creativity settings, you open yourself up to having some really interesting things happen. This is all about pushing your own limits and getting past the easy answers.

HOW TO DO IT:
1. Use up all 100 of the circles provided (or 100 circles that you draw first on your own paper) by either:
  a. drawing things where the circle is the outside shape (i.e., the sun) or
  b. drawing things where the circle is an inside shape (i.e., a hole in a tree).
2. Keep track of your time and be sure to finish within the one-hour time limit.
3. Document the things you discovered during this process in the space provided.

Start circling . . .

Keep circling . . .

NOTE: Don't use the circles as just a frame for drawing in. The idea is to make the circle part of the drawing.

Go all the way to 100 . . .

ALTERNATIVE: Work with a group of people to do this together. There's a very different set of experiences to be gained from doing this cooperatively.

What did you discover in the midst of all of those circles?

41

URBAN PHOTO SAFARI

Getting out of your comfort zone can be a scary prospect, but it's key to breaking mental barriers that are keeping you creatively confined. Often things aren't nearly as risky as they seem once you're doing them, and the benefits of putting yourself out there almost always far outweigh the potential for making a fool of yourself. The best way to get out of your comfort zone is to feel like it's something you have to do, rather than an option.

My friend Ben Hoffman runs a company called City Hunt (www.cityhunt.org) that does just that with their corporate clients. His team sends people around their own cities, requiring them to do a whole host of unusual activities that create long-lasting creative breakthroughs.

Treat this photographic scavenger hunt (in the spirit of Ben's City Hunt adventures) as something you've agreed to do and can't back out of.

HOW TO DO IT:

1. Using the list provided, see how many of these tasks you can accumulate in one hour. Some directions may seem impossible to achieve; see if you can find ways to solve them in ways that aren't entirely literal. And if something on the list seems especially daunting, try to do that first! The point is to do things that are a bit scary to you.

2. Document each task by photographing yourself doing it or by having someone else photograph you.

3. Keep track of the things you've accomplished and keep returning to the list over time until you've done them all.

4. Add new tasks to the list once you've gotten the hang of it!

TASKS

(including suggestions by Ben Hoffman):

1. Ask a stranger to tell you a story about their favorite pet.

2. Get a picture of yourself with a mannequin, then get a picture of yourself with the mannequin dressed in the same clothes as the mannequin.

3. Sing a song on a street corner.

4. Get a picture of yourself with Ben Franklin.

5. Get to a destination by only taking streets in ascending or descending alphabetical order.

6. Get a picture of yourself and four other people in midair.

7. Recreate a pose in a painting or statue directly in front of it.

8. Eat something from a can that has a language on it you can't read.

9. Dress up as someone you know and stand next to them.

10. Take a picture of five people underwater.

11. Have a meal with someone you don't know.

12. Get a picture of yourself giving a police officer a high five.

13. Get a photo of a table of people at a restaurant using their napkins as mustaches.*

14. Get a stranger to pick you up off the ground.

15. **Pretend to be talking on something other than a phone while you're walking down the street.**

16. **Ask a stranger to draw a portrait of you.**

17. **Ask to be included in a group photo being taken by tourists.**

18. **Wear your clothes backward and go for a walk.**

19. **Ask a stranger to help you play hide and seek.**

20. **Ask a stranger to give you a task to do.**

365 NAPKIN MUSTACHES

Phil Ford actually spent a year taking photos of himself using a napkin for a mustache during meals! He has plenty of great stories to go along with his experiences.

Read more about Phil's project here:

www.365napstache.blogspot.com

INSPIRATION

Document your safari finds here . . .

ALTERNATIVE: Get a group of people to do this at the same time. Work individually or, even better, in groups. You can even extend the time to make this an all-day event.

42

EVERY DAY IS

VALENTINES DAY

Creative inspiration can come from seeing the responses of others to your actions. My friend Paul Overton (see interview on page 92) came into an unexpected $100 and decided to spend it on a bit of unusual charity. He bought a $100 gift card at his local coffee shop and then handed it back to the cashier, saying, "The next hundred dollars in coffee is on me." The results of his action were later described by the staff as the equivalent of a "confusion grenade" being set off, as people's daily routines were shaken up in a surprising and positive way. This project is about creating a bit of your own happy confusion and seeing how it reverberates.

HOW TO DO IT:
1. Buy ten flowers or candy bars, pastries, cups of coffee, or other small, inexpensive items.
2. Give them to ten people that you wouldn't normally give a gift to.
3. Document their reactions in the space provided.
4. Document your own reactions in the space provided.

What did you give away? How did people react?

BONUS: Take a photo of yourself with the person you gave your gift to.

How did you feel? Document your own reaction here . . .

43

OFF
THE GRID

It's hard to imagine a time when we didn't use a variety of electronic tools to do work and communicate with one another. But it wasn't actually that long ago that every task was done without the need for electricity. Even though these tools are designed to make our lives easier, very often we spend more time doing mundane, noncreative things because of the technology we live with. Most of the projects in this book very intentionally ask you to do things that don't require a computer to complete them. That's because if you start with a tool, you'll only do what that tool can do, whereas if you start with your brain, you'll decide what to do and then find or make a tool that can get it done.

This task simply requires you to spend the next hour working without technology to remind yourself of what you have the potential to do.

HOW TO DO IT:

1. Turn off all electronic devices you are currently near. That includes phone, email, music, lights, etc.
2. Spend the next hour accomplishing as much of your normal work as you can. If you normally do work that doesn't require power, then challenge yourself to do other things in your life that would.
3. Document how you accomplished your tasks in the space provided and how you felt doing them.

ONE HOUR PROJECTS

How did you get things done?

How did the experience make you feel?

BONUS: Spend an entire day or weekend doing this.

MARK HURST is a writer and entrepreneur who helps people and businesses create good experiences.

CREATIVITY VS. THE INBOX

photo: Steve Worth

I'm going to teach you my own personal secret to being productive and making space for creative inspiration. You can achieve both, or at least begin the process, with one simple step. It's going to sound crazy, but hear me out.

The secret is to get your email inbox empty—I mean read and unread messages, everything, to a count of exactly ZERO—at least once a day. I don't mean that you have to delete all your email. You can still keep an archive, mail folders, whatever you want. Just zero the inbox.

I've been teaching people this method since the late 1990s, and it never fails to surprise and delight the people who put it into practice. Because most people face the same problem: emails pile up in the inbox and constantly call out for attention, and it's difficult to decide what to work on next. With hundreds or even thousands of competing priorities staring you in the face, it's hard to think clearly.

"Just zero the inbox."

Imagine the flip side: an empty inbox, no distractions, no competition for your attention. Nothing. You're liberated to think about other things than a mountain of old messages.

When I describe this to people for the first time, some claim that it's impossible. But I do, and lots of colleagues and readers of mine do. It's more than possible; it's actually somewhat simple.

The trick is to consider the contents of your inbox in three categories: stuff you don't need, stuff you might need to refer back to, and stuff that you need to take action on. The first category you can delete (no need to archive old lunch invites or spam messages). The second category you can stuff into whatever storage scheme you prefer; just get it out of the inbox. The last category—action items—move onto a to-do list (there are lots of great tools online to help with this*). And voilà: the inbox is empty.

Once you zero the inbox, you can much more easily choose what to work on next because all of your action items are in one place without irrelevant messages cluttering the view.

Taking the inbox from a cluttered mess to a pristine view of emptiness is a good analogy for the clarity you'll feel once you go through the process. Clear out the inbox and you'll see that your mind has more space to think bigger thoughts.

*Including Mark's own tool GoodTodo: **www.goodtodo.com**.

Mark Hurst *is the founder and host of the Gel Conference, an annual event spotlighting creative leaders from many different fields (www.gelconference. com). He also is the founder of the customer experience firm Creative Good, the author of the annual* Uncle Mark Gift Guide & Almanac, *and creator of the online to-do list, Good Todo.*

www.GoodExperience.com

CREATIVE ADVICE

SKILLS

GO WITH THE FLOW

ONE
HOUR
PROJECTS

Sometimes the best way to get creative is to switch gears and do something very technical for a while instead. At the very least, your mental resistance to this new task may jolt you back into creativity mode. However, the practice could also give you some insight into your working process and help you see more clearly the options you have.

HOW TO DO IT:

1. Choose a task that you do fairly regularly or know a lot about. This can be something mundane or silly, or it can even be something having to do with whatever you are currently working on.

2. Write down all of the steps and points at which you have to make decisions along the way.

3. Using the standard language of flow charts (see diagrams), lay out your task in the space provided or on your own paper.

4. Be sure to periodically try out the chart to see if it actually works. Imagine if you gave it to someone else to do. Would they be able to follow it and get a satisfactory result?

Start flowing here . . .

BONUS: Have other people try it out.

ALTERNATIVE: Diagram a task that involves movement by adding footprint images on your chart. Have people try it out.

SO YOU FOUND SOMETHING COOL ON THE INTERNET . . .

Comic artists Ross Nover and H. Caldwell Tanner created this fun flow chart to explain the ins and outs of sharing things on the Internet.

See more of their creations at:
www.systemcomic.com
and
www.loldwell.com

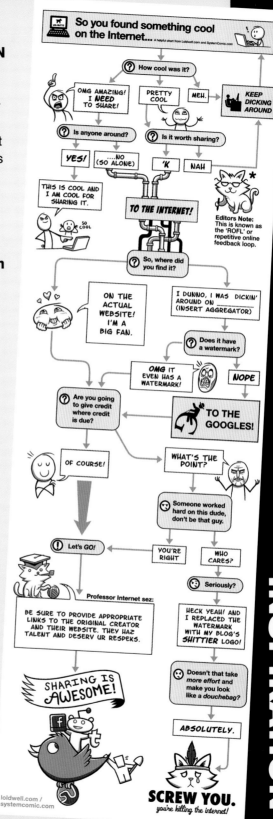

WISH YOU WERE HERE

Even though the standard way of sending words to someone is now mostly through digital means, there is a growing group of people who use the mail as a means of making and sending art. Mail art can be almost anything as long as it will get from one place to another through the postal system. Some artists even make their own custom stamps (which they use in addition to legitimate postage). This particular exercise is about not just making art but also making a connection using the art.

HOW TO DO IT:

1. Find the address of a friend or acquaintance you wish to do this project with. They can be informed in advance, or you can surprise them.

2. Get or make two postcards. They could be vintage ones, current souvenir ones from your hometown, or even just blank rectangles of cardboard (4.25" × 6" is the maximum mailable size at postcard rate in the United States). Odd-sized cards can be mailed but may need additional postage.

3. Modify one or both of the cards however you like. Add additional elements by gluing or painting them on, or cut or scratch away parts. Don't spend a ton of time on this; just have fun with it.

4. Mail both cards separately. Explain on one that this is for your friend to keep, and ask them to modify the other and send it back to you to keep. Be sure to document them before you send them off!

What did you put in the mail?

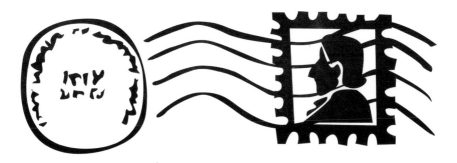

What did you get back in the mail?

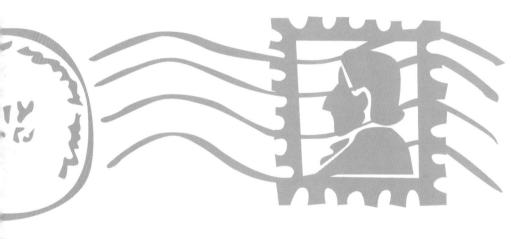

BONUS: Ask your friend to send you two postcards as well so you can do the same back to them! That way you both end up with two original pieces of art.

A YEAR OF MAIL ART

In 2010, London-based mail art aficionado Andy Hoang decided to corral a group of fellow mail artists and create Mailart365, in which more than thirty artists around the world took the challenge of making (and mailing) a piece of art every day for a year!

Shown below are several mail art pieces made by Mailart365 participant (and also my mom) Mim Golub. . . .

images: Mim Golub

See all of the works created on the group's site:

www.mailart365.blogspot.com

INSIDE
OUT

ONE
HOUR
PROJECTS

Many of the projects in this book require you to spend some time outside. That's because for the most part, people spend their time working and creating indoors and yet most of the interesting stuff is happening on the other side of their windows. While you can't always run outside to play when it's a lovely day, what if you could run outside and work? If there's a day you'd rather be outside, this is for you.

HOW TO DO IT:
1. Gather together enough of your working materials to spend a good hour working on a task that doesn't require electrical outlets.
2. Find a space outside of where you are currently working that is not directly in the way of pedestrians and set up shop.
3. Rather than just treat it like a working picnic, bring out some furniture so that it has a more office-like quality. See if you can quickly create a mini-version of your existing workspace, but don't spend too much time on this part.
4. Observe how the change of environment changes your attitude and emotions.
5. Interacting with curious onlookers is part of the experience so don't shy away from engaging with them.

What experiences did you have swapping inside for outside?

ALTERNATIVE: Celebrate your version of Park(ing) Day, an art holiday created by the people at Rebar, an art and design studio in San Francisco. They've designated the third Friday in September as a day for people to create outdoor parks in parking spaces in urban areas (paying the meter of course, if there is one). Get their advice about how to do this, and check out the instant parks that have already been created around the world on the group's site:

www.parkingday.org

photo: Ted Dewan

ROADWITCH

Roadwitching is a term coined by artist Ted Dewan for activities that take place on roads but use them for something other than purely vehicular traffic. What began as a prank to slow down traffic in his U.K. neighborhood so kids could trick-or-treat safely on Halloween became a series of experimental installations. In one case, Ted created an outdoor living room by putting a bunch of old furniture and a carpet on the street. It didn't take long for people in the neighborhood to start actually using the space and even adding their own touches to it. Eventually his experiments led to a legitimately sanctioned redesign of several city streets in England!

See more of Ted's experiments with Roadwitching here:

www.roadwitch.org.uk

INSPIRATION

ELIZABETH SMARTT is an author and freelance naming consultant.

STEPPING OUT

photo: Wayne Dement

When I worked as a naming consultant at FutureBrand in New York City, I had a cubicle. Most of the executives had spacious offices with windows overlooking Rockefeller Center, but my desk was in a dark corner surrounded by fabric dividers. I wasn't exposed to much natural light and had to swing my chair around 180 degrees to even see another human being. My work involved creative thinking. Clients depended on me and my boss to come up with effective, inspired, and legally available brand names for their companies and products.

Sometimes I had as many as ten or twelve clients at a time so it was a sort of creativity-under-fire situation. Staring up at the blah-beige fabric divider of my cubicle did nothing for my ability to generate names, and I kept getting stuck on the same ideas. So I pinned up a few photographs of the Blue Ridge Mountains, my friends and family, and an Einstein quote my boss told me about: "If at first, the idea is not absurd, then there is no hope for it." Still nothing.

I did everything I could think of to inspire my creativity. I bought a new thesaurus, a fascinating book called *The Way Things Work*, and some stress toys. I even bought a little bottle of aromatherapy lotion that promised to unlock my stress and release creativity. Finally, my boss, whom I continue to admire for his unconventional approach to tackling the corporate world, suggested that I get out of the office for inspiration.

I took the elevator downstairs and sat in the atrium by the big picture windows overlooking the ice skaters circling the rink. Watching the skates cut patterns into the ice as skaters swirled and laughed and held hands, I had the most productive afternoon generating names. It sounds too simple to work, but stepping out of my comfort zone (and the cubicle!) made a huge difference in spurring my creativity.

The hardest part was convincing my coworkers that I was working, not playing hooky. Once they realized that the quality of my creative work was higher when I left the office and found interesting spots to sit and observe the world from a different angle, it became part of my daily routine.

"It sounds too simple to work, but stepping out of my comfort zone (and the cubicle!) made a huge difference in spurring my creativity."

*Since 2001, **Elizabeth Thalhimer Smartt** has run her own freelance naming consultancy, Smartt Ideas, creating brand names for products and companies. Her client roster includes DuPont, Electrolux, Wachovia, and Cisco, among many others. Prior to freelancing, Elizabeth worked for branding agencies Landor Associates and FutureBrand. She graduated cum laude from Wake Forest University with a bachelor's degree in communication and a minor in theater, and earned a masters degree in English from Virginia Commonwealth University. In 2010, she published* Finding Thalhimers *(Dementi Milestone Publishing), chronicling five generations of her father's family and their beloved department store, Thalhimers, a Southern retail institution for 150 years. Elizabeth lives with her husband Ryan, daughter Lyla, and pug Deacon in Richmond, Virginia.*

www.findingthalhimers.com

CREATIVE ADVICE

SKILLS

SKILL SHED

Sometimes you just don't have the tools you need to get a job done. But usually if you ask around, a friend will lend you what you need. Wouldn't it be nice if you could do the same thing with creative skills?

Learning a new skill can be an amazing way to get inspired since it gives you a brand-new perspective on a material or a process. Plus, spending time learning from other creative people opens up a world of creative opportunities.

HOW TO DO IT:

1. Check off the skills you already have from the starter list and add your own in the space provided.

2. Circle the skills you want to learn and list people you know who could teach them to you (or at least help you do them).

3. If you don't know a person who can help you, find a local resource (school, business, organization) that you could turn to.

4. Choose one person or resource to make contact with today and set up a time to have them teach you something new.

5. Work your way through the rest of your list whenever you need a new tool in your own skill shed.

Start filling your shed . . .

SKILLS

☐ Woodworking

☐ Woodcarving

☐ Glassblowing

☐ Metalsmithing

☐ Jewelry making

☐ Graphic design

☐ Beadmaking

☐ Life drawing

☐ Pastels

☐ Oil painting

☐ Watercolor

☐ Photography

☐ Pottery

☐ Writing fiction

☐ Writing nonfiction

☐ Printmaking

☐ Ceramic sculpture

☐ Quilting

☐ Sewing

☐ Knitting

☐ Stained glass

☐ Silk screening

☐ Playing an instrument (list)

☐ Welding

☐ Encaustic painting

☐ Glass fusing & slumping

☐ Videography

☐ Cartooning

☐ Construction

☐ Fashion design

☐ Weaving

☐ Interior design

Add your own here . . .

BRAIN PARTY

When I set out to write this book, I knew there was no way I would be able to come up with fifty-two projects out of thin air, nor did I want to! One of the first things I did was just talk to my friends about what I was doing, and immediately people started suggesting ideas. But the process really kicked off when one friend suggested that we get a group of friends together to talk about it as a group one night. I ended up with dozens of ideas, many of which ended up in this book. Brainstorming is a common creative tool, but too often it's restricted to work settings and done in a structured format. It doesn't need to be that formal; it's really just about getting things out of your head and sharing them with others.

HOW TO DO IT:

1. Invite a small but diverse group of friends to join you for breakfast, lunch, or dinner at your workspace or somewhere where it's okay to be raucous. Try to include people who don't necessarily already do what you do.

2. You can make it a potluck or you can provide your own food. I bought two pizzas, and that small investment made for a lot of happy people. The key is having food and letting people know you won't just be hanging out like normal.

3. Start by describing what you're currently working on and where you're stuck. Then just listen to what people say, and write their ideas down in the space provided. It won't take long for people to start bouncing ideas off each other.

4. Enforce a no "naysaying" rule on yourself. All ideas, even the most improbable, are valid starting points. You never know where they'll lead.

5. After an hour at most, let the topic of your project go. The group can disperse or continue on as a non-structured party if you like.

How was the party? Write down your friends' ideas here . . .

Keep brainstorming . . .

ALTERNATIVE: Have some one-on-one brainstorming meals with friends (your treat, of course). I had creative breakfasts and lunches with many of my friends while writing this book and never left without one or more great ideas to work on that day!

MULTⓍ HOUR PROJECTS

TIME MACHINE

49

Sometimes new ideas come from old ones.
Spending time thinking about other moments in your life can get you thinking in all kinds of different ways. This exercise is based on the Young Me/Now Me project by the amazingly inspiring Ze Frank. It's about paying attention to details and recreating the past in a way that will inspire you today.

HOW TO DO IT:

1. Choose an old photo of yourself. It can be you alone, or if you want to do this with others, it can be a group shot.

2. Find or make clothing, props, and a location that look like the one in the photo. They can even be the originals if they still exist.

3. Put yourself in the scene and, either using a timer or with the help of someone else, take a photo of you in the same pose with the same expression.

MULT⌛
HOUR
PROJECTS

Document your time travel experience here:

ALTERNATIVE: Choose someone else's old photo to recreate or even a painting or other work of art.

BONUS: Write a bit about the original photo, why you chose to recreate it, and how the experience affected you.

YOUNG ME, NOW ME

For tons of inspiration and to share your own photos, visit Ze Franks's Young Me/Now Me site:
www.zefrank.com/youngmenowme/blog

My sister and I created this submission for the Young Me, Now Me project in an afternoon. The hardest part was finding the yellow raincoat, so we ended up using a yellow hoodie from the thrift store instead.

And visit Ze's site for plenty of other creative projects:

www.zefrank.com

50

URBAN ALPHABET

Once you start really looking, it's hard not to see all kinds of unexpected things in your environment. This is a project my father taught to his art students for many years. It helps hone your observational skills to a fine point by discovering the entire alphabet hiding around you. You can use this as a way to thoroughly investigate the areas where you spend most of your time. Or this can be an excuse to travel out of your usual circles. Why not even spend the day on a bicycle since it's easier to get off and on when you spot something that would work?

HOW TO DO IT:

1. Cut the square out at right so you can use the book as a viewfinder.

2. With camera in hand, head outside to begin your search. (A cell phone camera is perfectly acceptable if you don't have an alternate option.)

3. With the shapes of the letters in your mind, start looking around for places where lines are formed by the outside edges of objects, by the spaces between objects, and/or by a combination of the two.

4. Use your viewfinder (or hands) to help hide extraneous imagery and focus in on your discoveries.

5. When you take your photos, try to fill as much of the image as possible with the letter.

6. There's no need to do this in order; just use the check boxes at right to note when you've found a letter. This also makes it easy to pick up the project again if you want to stop and restart on another day.

Pareidolia: Seeing a meaningful pattern in something that is random or ambiguous (seeing a face on the surface of the moon, for example).

BONUS: Take the letters you've found, use them to spell out your name or other words, and use them in your work or as decoration.

ALTERNATIVE: Try looking for the numbers 0–9 instead or as well!

List your finds from point A to point Z . . .

☐ **A**

☐ **B**

☐ **C**

☐ **D**

☐ **E**

☐ **F**

☐ **G**

☐ **H**

☐ **I**

☐ **J**

☐ **K**

☐ **L**

☐ **M**

- [ ] N

- [ ] O

- [ ] P

- [ ] Q

- [ ] R

- [ ] S

- [ ] T

- [ ] U

- [ ] V

- [ ] W

- [ ] X

- [ ] Y

- [ ] Z

WRITING IN THE SKY

Check out the beautiful letterforms discovered between buildings by designer Lisa Reinermann:

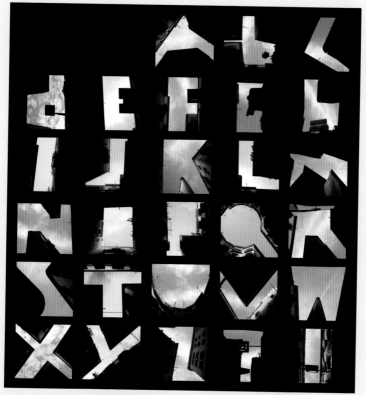

See more of Lisa's work here:

www.lisareinermann.com

INSPIRATION

LOST ART

When artist Tiffany Glass Ferreira was looking to feel more inspired about her work, she decided to give it away to strangers. After posting a piece on a community bulletin board (with her email address on the back), she got an immediate and positive response. This inspired her to start the Real Small Art League (www. realsmallart.blogspot.com), which encourages other artists to gain the benefits of "random acts of artistic kindness and creative awareness" by putting work in public places to be found by others.

Taking a cue from Tiffany, this exercise is all about gaining from giving away.

HOW TO DO IT:

1. Make ten or so small items with whatever materials you have on hand. These can be all different or variations on a theme. Don't spend a lot of time on these; this is not about perfection. They're meant to inspire, not create further pressure! Even small drawings on sticky notes will work.*

*One caveat: Tiffany has found that the response was much bigger if things seemed like something one might buy, rather than just a piece of paper. Her preferred medium of choice is a tiny stretched canvas painting.

2. Include an email address or website directly on the piece or a tag attached to it so people can contact you when they find your piece. If you're worried about giving out personal information, it's easy to set up a free email account especially for this project on Gmail, Yahoo, etc. Websites take more time to set up if you don't have one already, but if you have decided this is something you want to keep doing, it might be worth setting up a free blog (using Blogger, WordPress, Posterous, Tumblr, etc.) specifically for it.

3. Head out with your items and leave them in places where they won't be immediately considered litter or vandalism. You can go to your usual haunts so that you can return to see how long it takes for them to be found or go on a special trip to new places specifically to distribute your items. Tiffany suggests using places that are already considered "point of information exchanges," such as coffee shop bulletin boards, for the best response.

4. Document the places you've left things with photos and/or by writing in the spaces provided.

ALTERNATIVE: Do this when you travel to other cities or countries. It can make sharing travel photos much more exciting.

Where did you last see your art?

LOST CATS

Alyson Plante and L. Campbell Maxey are members of the Real Small Art League. They make tiny ceramic cats, which they leave around Richmond, Virginia. Their website includes a Lost & Found Gallery that allows people to see where cats have been left behind and who has adopted them!

photos: Alyson Plante and L. Campbell Maxey

www.lostcats.wordpress.com

SMELL YOU LATER A.K.A. SCENT LIBRARY

It's well known that our sense of smell is intimately connected with our memories. One whiff of a particular scent can instantly transport you back to a different time and place in your life. Need to get in the mood to create something about winter in summer? Need to recall what it was like to be in school for the first time? Need to remember how you feel when you're relaxing on a beach? Taking the time to build a scent library now could give you lots of opportunities for taking advantage of this connection between smell and memory to gain creative inspiration when you need it! Plus the activity of doing this project alone will give you a chance to pour over old memories that may jog all kinds of new thoughts.

HOW TO DO IT:
1. Take some time to think about and write out a list of scents that bring back memories for you in the space provided.
2. Pick out a few that represent a wide range of experiences and emotions, focusing especially on ones that can be reproduced with items you can attain fairly easily (i.e., pencil shavings for a classroom memory).
3. Find or buy a small set of airtight jars. Thoroughly cleaned spice jars could work well if they don't retain any of the scent from their previous contents.
4. Fill the jars with the appropriate items for the smells you want to collect, and label them with the memories they evoke.
5. Keep the jars in a handy place so they can be grabbed at a moment's notice. Refill them as their scents fade.

Make your list of scents and their associated memories here:

BONUS: Make these with friends and then share your memories and scents. Maybe you'll discover some new memories of your own!

TYPES OF ITEMS TO INCLUDE:
Dirt
Sand
Dried flowers
Spices and herbs
A small amount of perfume
  or essential oil
Burnt matches
Vinegar
Coffee beans or tea leaves
Pencil shavings
Shampoo/soap
Sawdust
Dryer lint

Experiment and see if you can get hard-to-capture scents by combining items. Make sure items are fairly shelf-stable or you could end up with the smell of mold instead of what you expected.

CUT-OUTS

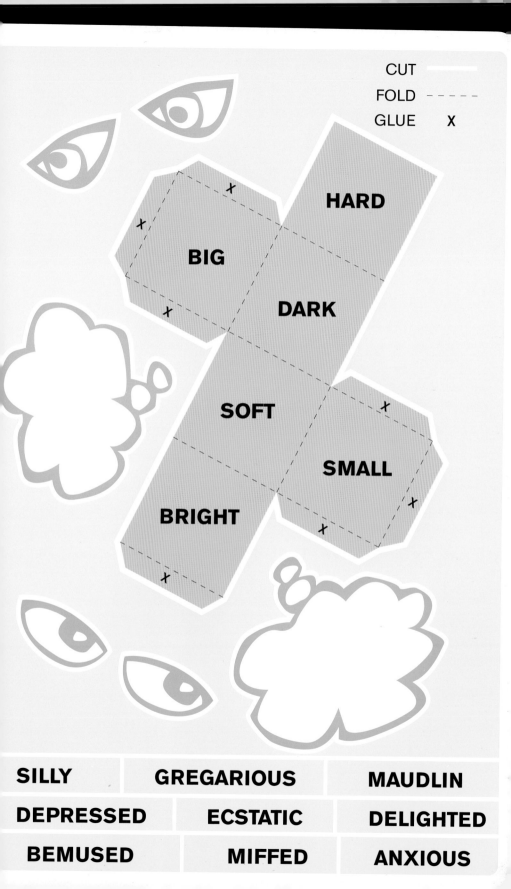

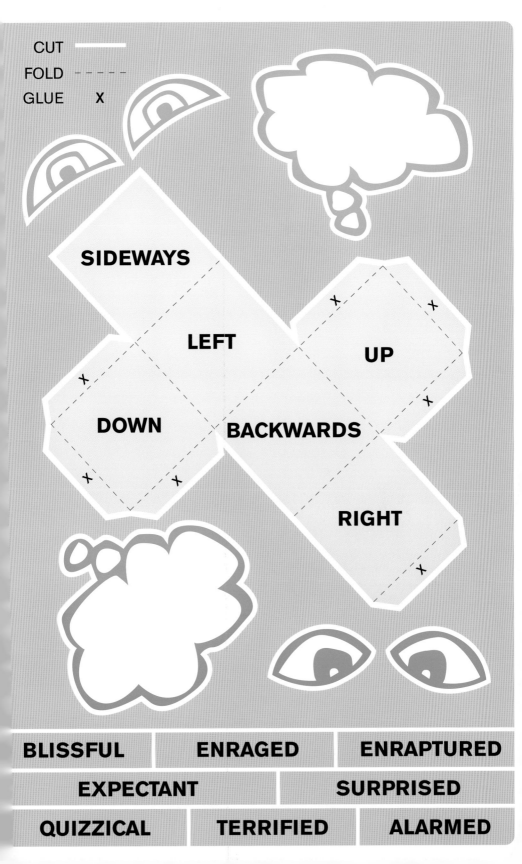

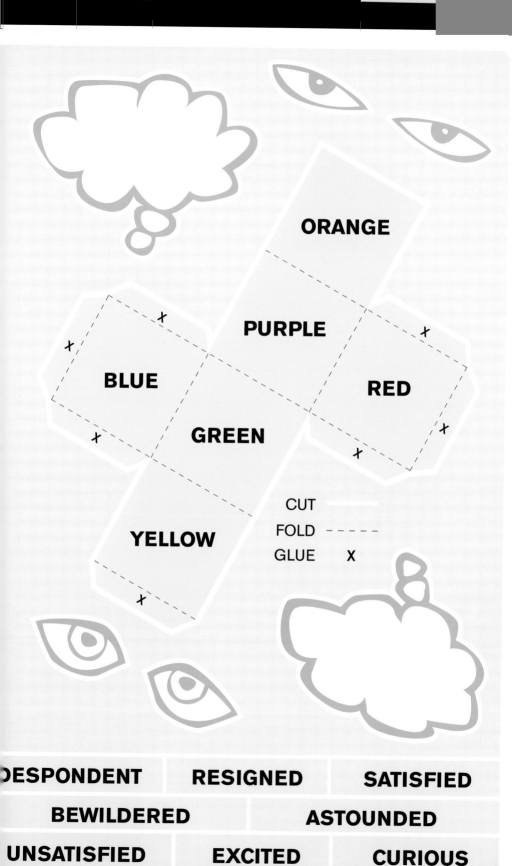

FROM A DAY TO A WEEK TO A YEAR
Taking things to the next level

There's a secret about this book: it's actually a yearlong project in disguise! For many people, a daily project is such an overwhelming task that they'll never get started on it. But what if you've already started and haven't even realized it? Here's my challenge to you:

Why not just start using this book when you feel stuck, but then keep doing one exercise a week for the next fifty-one weeks after that?

That doesn't sound so bad does it? There are exactly fifty-two projects so you can mark them off as you go and easily keep track of your progress! And before you know it you'll have accomplished a yearlong project of your own.

And for a greater challenge, you can even try doing each project seven times each and suddenly you'll be doing a daily creative project!

For plenty of inspiration on the topic, check out the 365 projects that people are doing all over the world via my site:

MakeSomething365.com

MORE SOURCES OF INSPIRATION?

Sometimes, too much inspiration is just as bad as not enough.
Sprinkled throughout this book are a whole host of interesting people
and projects to check out online. But be careful. It's very easy to
spend your creative time just looking at what other people have
accomplished. And instead of feeling excited about starting your own
projects, you suddenly feel like you'll never be as good as they are or
accomplish as much as they have. The key is making sure you spend
more time creating than you are consuming. Whenever you feel
overwhelmed by the things other people have done, immediately start
doing something of your own—even a tiny amount—and the progress
you make will add up to something much bigger.

ACKNOWLEDGMENTS

The Anti-Coloring Book by Susan Striker and Edward Kimmel was a seminal part of my childhood. In many ways, *Unstuck* is the tree that grew from the seed that those authors planted in me and was cultivated by my parents watering it with their constant support and encouragement.

This book would absolutely not exist if it weren't for my wonderful friends and family, who gave me so much help and inspiration throughout the process: Chelsea Kostek, Eliza Skinner, Carra Rose, Karen Mullins, Andy Stefanovich, Tere Hernández-Bonét, Meena Khalili Clifford, Amy McFadden, Matthew Lively, Slash Coleman, Spencer Hansen, Michael Harl, Matt Deans, Nathan Wender, Tiffany Glass Ferreira, Leah Lamb, Juliette Christine, Madonna Dersch, Caryn Persinger, Bernadine Jones, and all of the other wonderful creative people who took the time to share their own stories of getting unstuck . . . Thank you!

And my deepest appreciation goes out to . . .

Margret Aldrich, Michael Dregni, Catherine Steen, Danielle Ibister, and all of the fine folks at Voyageur Press who have been such kind collaborators.

Kate McKean, who has not just been my agent but also a friend.

My sister Mica who has been the constant, creative, co-conspirator throughout my life.

My parents, Mim and Chuck, who are the best creative role models anyone could ask for.

And Jessica, who has more creative energy than anyone I know!

ABOUT YOU

_____

_____

_____

_____

_____

_____

_____

_____

_____

ABOUT THE AUTHOR

Noah Scalin is an artist, designer, and activist based in Richmond, Virginia. He created the Webby Award–winning daily art project Skull-A-Day (www.skulladay.com), which led to his first two books: _Skulls_ and _365: A Daily Creativity Journal_. His fine art has been exhibited in museums and galleries internationally, including the Mütter Museum in Philadelphia and the International Museum of Surgical Science in Chicago. Noah also founded the internationally recognized, socially conscious design and consulting firm Another Limited Rebellion. Noah teaches a course on socially conscious design at Virginia Commonwealth University, and he frequently lectures and leads workshops on creativity for everyone from teenagers in New York City to designers in the CIA.

www.NoahScalin.com

Noah Scalin. _photo: Mark Mitchell_